Best and Fairest Sports Parenting

Published by Melbourne Books
Level 9, 100 Collins Street,
Melbourne, VIC 3000
Australia
www.melbournebooks.com.au
info@melbournebooks.com.au

Title: Best and Fairest Sports Parenting
Author: Nathan Burke
ISBN: 9781922779045

Front cover image: Nathan Burke and his daughter. (Photo by Michael Willson/AFL Photos)
Back cover image: Former St Kilda player and AFL Hall of Fame inductee Nathan Burke poses with wife Fiona and daughters Alice, Ruby and Milly during a photo shoot at home in Melbourne, Victoria, 2021. (Photo by David Caird / Newspix)
Inside front cover image: Nathan Burke and father Barry. (Photo: Burke family)

A catalogue record for this book is available from the National Library of Australia

Best and Fairest Sports Parenting

NATHAN BURKE

M
MELBOURNE BOOKS

Contents

Sports Parenting

How to get your kids to love you and sport at the same time

I grew up in a Housing Commission estate in Frankston North—the Pines, to be more exact. The local police more colloquially called it 'The Bronx'. There were my three older sisters; twins Kerryn and Vicki, Martene; and me, the youngest. My father Barry was a floor tiler and local football legend while Glenys was your stereotypical stay-at-home mum. Our grandmother also lived with us, which made seven of us in a three-bedroom housing commission home.

My fondest childhood memories are not of long hot summers at the beach, but wintry Saturdays spent at the local Australian Rules Football. My father played and coached at various times for the Pines Pythons and the Clayton Magpies in suburban Melbourne football competitions.

Saturday was always match day, where Dad would leave early to get things set up while we would stay behind to enjoy a warming bowl of soup and toast soldiers layered with butter. My mum, sisters and I would tag along later that day, always resplendent in our team colours.

To the team members and supporters of the clubs, I was 'Lil Burkey', and despite my red hair and freckles clashing badly with the red and green of the Pythons, I thought I looked pretty cool dressed just like the players.

Upon arriving at the ground I was off—'See ya later, Mum, be back when the siren goes.' If I was lucky, I would be asked to look after the scoreboard, for which my reward would be a twenty-cent bag of lollies and can of Coke. If not, I would easily find ways to amuse myself by climbing trees, playing on the swings, or kicking the ball that was always in my hand. Local sporting clubs are the lifeblood of many communities and I feel fortunate to have grown up in such an environment. Basically, Mum didn't need to keep an eye on me every second because there were countless other club members ready and willing to step in if they saw anything untoward.

To say that it was sports-loving house would be an understatement. For me it was the traditional sports of football in winter, cricket in summer, and basketball seemed to go year-round. For my sisters it was netball, basketball, and something called calisthenics. Though, purely to annoy my sisters, I refused to call calisthenics a sport.

Our lives revolved around our sports and, looking back now, getting each of us to our respective games and trainings must have been a logistical nightmare. The relaxed road laws that allowed Dad to round up half a dozen kids and throw them in the back of his work van (where we sat on upturned buckets) certainly helped get everyone where we needed to be.

It is during this time that I became aware of parental influences on a child and their sporting endeavours.

To say my father was involved is an understatement. At various times he coached my junior football team before eventually going on to become President of the club. He also coached my basketball team before going on to become President of the basketball club and then President of the whole basketball association.

Now you may well be thinking that he is one of those extreme sports parents who are over-involved in their kids' sports. Certainly all the initial signs were there. He was a footballer who played reserve level at Richmond, won a Premiership with Sandringham in Victoria's second-tier competition, didn't have a father figure in his own life, and had three daughters before a footballing prospect son came along. It all points in the right direction, doesn't it?

But the truth is my father was almost the perfect model of a supportive sports parent. I say *almost* because he did have a love-hate relationship with umpires and referees that occasionally went a tad too far—a trait I am not proud to say I may have inherited during certain occasions in my younger days. I also know that, at times, he may have spent money that he didn't have to make sure we never went without anything.

As much as I wanted new boots at the start of every season like some of the other kids, I understood the importance of making them last. In fact this was one of the earliest sporting lessons he ever taught me: 'If you are going to be a footballer, you have to look like one.' That meant polishing your boots before every game, tucking your shirt in, and making sure your socks were pulled up. And he would rather undergo a root canal than miss a game or event his kids were involved in.

However, apart from these idiosyncrasies, he was the dad many of the other kids wanted to have. Especially the kids who he would round up and throw in the back of his van to get to games. And the ones who slept on the floor of our motel room just so they could get to play in the basketball tournament. And, especially, the ones whose parents were never on the sidelines.

I was comforted some years later when I found out that he had taken on the Presidency of the Long Island Lawn Bowls club after only six months of membership. He assured me the reason why he took it on was because, like all the other times, no-one else would do it. He later admitted to the fact that he has an in-built desire to see things done correctly and can't stand to 'sit by and see things done half arsed'. I have no doubt this is what made him such a good floor tiler for over fifty years until his knees gave way.

Despite four kids playing all over the place, Dad and Mum never missed an opportunity to be on the sidelines to support us. It was this constant presence more than anything else that got me interested in the concept of ideal sports parenting. I was acutely aware that other kids' parents weren't as involved as mine, and many of the kids seemed okay with that. They played for fun and weren't concerned that their parents weren't there supporting them.

Around the age of fifteen you start to get a bit self-conscious, and I began to think about the level of involvement my parents had in my sports and life. I began to ponder many questions.

Did I need to have my parents around so much? Was it uncool for them to always be there? Just by being there, were my dad and mum putting added pressure on me to play well? Was I constantly trying to impress them? Did I play for fun like the other kids? What would they have thought if I said I didn't want to play anymore? What would happen if I got older and didn't stand out as much as I used to? What if I didn't realise the potential everyone said I had—would they still be involved?

My answers to these questions came from observing what happened as my two eldest sisters grew. Both were good sportswomen but neither quite made the grade when it came to significant representative sides in basketball or netball. It was becoming clear that being very good local players would be the highest level they would reach in their chosen sports.

I paid particular attention to how my parents reacted to this situation. Would the level of involvement and enjoyment they had in their daughters' sports drop off? Would the added focus then be placed on me and Martene to improve and succeed, as we both seemed to be on a more elite pathway at the time?

The answer was nothing changed. Mum and Dad remained just as involved with my two eldest sisters as they were with me and Martene. This was despite the fact that we were starting to progress up the junior ranks; me in football and Martene in basketball; which meant a heavier training and time commitment for each of us.

Seeing my parents derive as much enjoyment out of Kerryn and Vicki playing at local level was like a monkey being lifted off my back. They were beside us all the way because they loved it. They loved seeing us have fun. They loved seeing us participate in well-managed sports and could honestly say they just wanted us to play. They loved seeing us compete but never focused too much on winning. They wanted to give us every opportunity to succeed; not for them, but for us. And in the end, whether we succeeded or not didn't come down to whether we made a career out of sport, but whether we reached our potential. If that potential meant playing 300 AFL games, then great. If it meant winning B-Grade Ladies Summer Comp at Frankston, then equally great.

It is these examples that ignited my passion for helping parents and coaches of junior sport provide the best environment for kids to play. I firmly believe that every coach and parent wants what is best for their kids. It's just that some go about it in a misguided fashion whilst others can't find the help they need.

I need to make the point that by no means have my wife and I been perfect parents—no-one is. We look back now and recognise the mistakes that we made; all well-meaning of course, but mistakes nonetheless. You will see that many of my examples come from real life stuff-ups. There were times when we verged on being poisonous sports parents—not only infecting our kids but those around us also. The most important thing is that we realised our mistaken ways pretty quickly and to this day have a great relationship with our kids, who tell us they still love us.

Many years as a sports kid and now a sports parent to three teenage daughters has given me the experience and wisdom to know where the line is when it comes to being over-involved or under-involved. Just like my parents before me, my wife Fiona and I derive great joy from watching our daughters Ruby, Molly and Alice giving their all on the field. Truth be told, I get as much joy out of watching them as I did in seventeen years of playing for the Saints. I know my wife enjoys it more, although her constant worry over injury and poor form has transferred from me to the kids.

The title of this book uses the words 'Best and Fairest Sports Parenting' because that is what we should set out to achieve. We shouldn't be parents who set out to make our children be successful; to have long careers and earn millions of bucks. The fact is, if we are the best parents that we can be, then your child will achieve what their potential allows them to achieve. And in the end, isn't that our overall job as parents? Importantly and most significantly, no matter what level they reach, they will maintain a loving, healthy and respectful relationship with you, their parents. That relationship is worth more than any gold medal or trophy they pick up along the way.

These days the greatest joy my parents get is standing on the sidelines watching their grandkids play sport. Whether it is getting up at 2.30am to watch their grandson Mitchell play US college basketball on their iPad, or standing in the rain to watch their grandchildren play U/13 soccer, they love it.

I dedicate this book to all the members of my family—the ones who guided me as a little red-haired kid, and my wife and kids who give me more joy than any sports field can offer. Thank you all for showing me the vital role supportive families play in raising happy, healthy, well-rounded kids who grow to have a lifelong love of sport.

Introduction

We've all seen them and we've definitely all heard them. No matter what sport your kid plays you will come across them at some stage during the year. They are of course, the *sideline psychos*. You probably know one and you may even be one. At their best they are embarrassing and at their worst they are damaging. We all feel sorry for their kids and wonder about what the relationship is like at home, or what it will be if the child doesn't become a star.

The damage these parents can do is limitless. In the worst case they can severely affect a child's self-esteem to the point where it leaves psychological scars. Even the mild cases, where the child might just give up and leave the sport altogether, can still harmful.

While the latter may seem like a lesser concern, if that child grows up to avoid sports altogether, then the likelihood of developing health concerns such as obesity through a sedentary lifestyle can be just as upsetting as mental scars. You may also find that your relationship with your child is irreconcilably damaged.

Look at any world sport and you will see a litany of examples where players, some who have even 'made the grade' at the top level, do not have a parent or family to share it with due to their fractured childhood relationships. And these are just the high-profile cases we know about because the player 'made it'. What about all the other parent-child relationships that have been broken that we *don't* know about because the child never realised their full potential?

Most likely we have never heard of these athletes because they gave up the sport too early or couldn't cope with the mental and physical pressure applied by the poisonous sports parent.

To get us started, here are some extreme examples of especially poisonous sports parents:

Christophe Fauviau

Although Christophe Fauviau's son and daughter have not become world-class players, he deserves a spot on in the Poison Parents Hall of Fame.

Fauviau doped the drinks of at least twenty-seven players during their matches against his son and daughter between 2000 and 2003. He was sentenced to jail in 2006 on a manslaughter conviction after one of the drugged players died in a car crash.

He said he had become obsessed with the tennis careers of his children while they played in junior tournaments in France.

Although only one drugged player died, others collapsed or became ill during matches, according to the BBC report. One was eleven years old.[1]

Stefano Capriati

Whether it was deserved or not, Stefano Capriati was blamed for many of the problems his daughter, Jennifer Capriati, had in her career and life.

The media charged him with treating Jennifer as his meal ticket, pushing her into the spotlight at an early age. She turned pro at thirteen and was getting major endorsement deals at fourteen.

Capriati left the tour at age eighteen and was later cited for shoplifting and arrested for marijuana possession. She entered a drug and alcohol rehabilitation facility that same year.[2]

Marinko Lucic

Father of Mirjana Lucic, Marinko was voted the worst tennis father ever in a 2003 poll by a British newspaper.

He was accused of being physically and mentally abusive, and Mirjana Lucic eventually fled to the United States to escape.

'Beatings ... there have been more of them than anyone can imagine,' Lucic, then sixteen, told a Zagreb newspaper, *Slobodna Dalmacija*, according to Associated Press.[3]

Now I'm tipping that you are nowhere near as bad as some of these examples but it's best to do a thorough self-assessment before you get to the point of no return.

I believe every parent genuinely wants to do the right thing by their children. The problem occurs when we aren't exactly sure what the right thing to do *is*. What is too much interest and what is not enough interest when it comes to children's sport? It's a dilemma many parents struggle with.

To assist, I have identified the areas you need to consider when assessing your sports parenting. If you identify with an issue, don't worry. For each 'issue', we will give you some simple alternative courses of 'action'—all of which can be acted upon with a little bit of effort and a lot of self-control. At the end of each chapter, we will summarise the key points, so when you need to come back for a refresher (and you will), you won't have to re-read the entire chapter.

Keep in mind the end goal, which is to help your child reach their potential while always maintaining a loving and respectful parent-child relationship that will last as long as you do.

Chapter 1

Issue: You place all of your emphasis on winning

Do you place all your emphasis on winning?

It isn't really how they play the game, but whether they win or lose that matters? Or do you just simply talk more about winning and rarely about improving?

If this is you … you may have an issue.

But hold on—is wanting to win that bad?

Isn't winning part of sport and, indeed, part of life? I know that I have often been described as a competitive person. Certainly in my football career, the word 'competitive' was used to describe me far often than the word 'skilful'. My three sisters will tell you that from an early age I had a reputation as a cheat whenever we played a board game. This wasn't because I was a naturally deceptive person—it was because I wanted to win. And I think I turned out okay, so what is wrong with wanting to win?

Let's explore this concept further.

Despite varied opinions on the subject, becoming a winner may be one of the most important things a person can do in their lifetime. If we devalue winning, then we can say goodbye to an enormous amount of untapped talent and capacity that will never surface to benefit humanity or enable people to experience being the best that they can be. If we give up on pursuing our goals and ambitions, it's equivalent to turning our backs on our birth talents and the privilege of life. Therefore, one of our highest and most honourable obligations we have as parents is to teach our kids to be winners.

In order to win, we must compete.

Personally I am an advocate for competition and can see numerous benefits of organised competition for children.

Here are just a few … eleven, in fact:

1. **Competition teaches us to bring our best effort,** and keeping score gives us extra motivation to do our best. We pursue excellence when we compete. There is nothing wrong with giving your best effort and indeed it is a necessary life skill. This is especially relevant for female athletes who sometimes feel uncomfortable about giving their best effort—they can become self-conscious and not want to be seen as too competitive for fear of being labelled a 'bitch'. They can also be more attuned to other women's feelings and 'pull back' so as not to make others feel bad. Many top female athletes will have had to overcome these issues.

2. **Competition teaches us to manage our nerves.** When something is out of our comfort zone or pushes us to perform, it's normal to feel fluttery inside. Competition brings those butterflies out, which allows us to practice managing them. The tactics you use to overcome your nerves can be the same tactics you use when going into an exam or a job interview later in life. The way you prepare for a game, do the hard work, practice, and continually improve are the same actions that will get you that good exam score.

3. **Competition does not have to be feared.** Often kids fear competition, making it into something scarier or more important than it needs to be. When they compete, they realise that it wasn't so scary after all. And let's not forget that competition is present in all aspects of life—at school, when they go for a job, when they are in the job, and even when they're attracting a significant other. If we shy away from competition, we shy away from life.

4. **Competition teaches us to cope when things do not go our way.** Sometimes you work hard, and still lose. Sometimes you win but still didn't perform as well as you wanted to. We learn resilience and grit in these moments—two traits that are most certainly essential in adulthood. I've seen many kids reach the age of sixteen or higher, then leave a sport the minute the competition gets too tough. Often this is because they have had a false sense of what sport is about as a junior. They never lost or had to strive to win and, as such, never learned the accompanying lessons. These lessons in loss are vital when they start to reach older levels of sport, where participation awards are replaced by ladders and scoreboards.

5. **Competition helps us with goal-setting.** Although setting goals and making a plan to reach them can be done outside of competition, competition helps provide deadlines and progress checks on those goals. Any person will tell you that a key component of goal-setting is *measurement*. I'm not just talking about wins and losses here, but also potentially losing by less points than you lost previously or winning by more points than you won previously. These measurements can be indicators as to whether your training is paying off, whether you need to change your plans and even how much time you need to put into your sport. Sport and competing also allows goals to be attained in a relatively short period of time—in the space of one season, large gains can be made with the appropriate work ethic.

6. **Competition teaches us to play by rules.** Learning to operate within rules and developing strategies to use those rules to our

advantage are great things competition teaches. The concept of 'fair play' is underrated and whilst we describe the adult world as dog-eat-dog and survival of the fittest, there is still room for ethical behaviour. Teaching a young golfer to apply a penalty stroke on herself and risk losing the match will have greater life repercussions than applying a penalty stroke in a match that doesn't mean anything or has no winners and losers.

7. **Competition helps us to learn to win and lose with grace.** Nobody likes a boastful person and nobody likes a sook. Competition gives us the opportunities to cope with feelings of pride and disappointment and to learn to process them in healthy ways. Without competing, how do you learn to win or lose with grace and honour? And don't tell me ten-year-old kids who have been told time and time again that 'there is no scoreboard' don't keep a mental note of who is winning or losing. Of course they do—so why not teach them how to do it properly?

8. **Competition is fun.** Most people enjoy games. Whether it is *Hungry Hungry Hippos*, table tennis or *Monopoly*, they have fun playing them. Should you tip the board over when it looks like one person is going to win so that no-one wins? Managed correctly, competition is fun for kids. In many kids, competing is a natural instinct that, on one hand, we say is a great characteristic to have and will help them in later life. On the other hand, we say they *shouldn't* be exposed to competition. It's confusing for them and for us.

9. **Competition can build self-esteem.** Self-esteem cannot be handed to kids; they have to earn it. Competition is one way kids earn self-esteem. When you develop a talent and work hard for a result, it feels great. When you fail and learn that you can bounce back, you feel more confident in yourself because you understand that you have resilience. Plus, sports-based self-esteem is derived from actual events; not mum and dad telling you how fantastic you are and possibly filling you full of unrealistic expectations. Not everyone can sing, for example. It's just a fact.

10. **Competition teaches commitment.** There is a saying that goes, 'Successful people do the things that unsuccessful people don't want to do. That is why they are successful.' Building the habit of commitment is a wonderful by-product of being involved in competitive sports. I also believe that 'match day is the greatest lie detector of all'. If you don't train and aren't committed, then you will be found out. Sport teaches this lesson well.

11. **Competition gives us another community.** When you are part of a team, you belong to a network of peers and adults who have interests and values similar to yours. Being part of a team or squad can help you feel like you belong. It is always great to have another village in your life, or in your child's life.

Considering the above, why do we still have a groundswell movement of people who are trying their darnedest to eradicate competition from junior sport? All over Australia there are examples of leagues and teams banning scoreboards, trophies and awards. In 2015 the AFL initiated a 'no scoreboard or B&F policy' with all junior leagues and teams in the U/8 and U/9 levels with a graduation to U/10 in coming years. There are also no finals, no ladders, no match scoring (they must hope that U/10s can't count yet) and no players' names published. These rules came on the back of quotes like 'kids play to have fun; they don't just play to win'.

What's that about the bleatingly obvious, I hear you say?

The anti-compete crowd will tell you that without a scoreboard the kids play purely for the joy of kicking a ball around, being with their friends and simply having fun. Absolutely they play for these reasons, but I will ask this question—what is *fun*?

Isn't it fun to test yourself against an opponent and triumph? If the answer is yes, then why do we put limits on the ways a child can have fun?

Think back to our *Monopoly* example—would you tip the board over as soon as your child was going to win? No, you wouldn't. You would finish the game and teach the lesson on how to win or lose gracefully.

So why do we shy away from it on the sports field? Why is winning at *Hungry Hungry Hippos* different from winning a tennis match?

The reason is because the adults can't cope. If a team of ten-year-olds continue to push and harass a team even though they are ten goals in front, it isn't the kids' fault. I guarantee you it is the coach's fault, and likely the over-competitive parents' fault, too. And if the kids are the ones pushing then they do so only because an adult has let them do it.

The anti-compete crowd will also point out that players won't develop the appropriate level of skills if they are too concerned with making a mistake that may cost their team the game. I have seen kids play within their capability by thinking too much about the bigger picture of winning and losing, or potentially letting their team down. It happens quite frequently and it does have the ability to stifle progress. So what do we do?

Well, we have two choices: We can take away any consequences (the scoreboard) and encourage the child to make as many mistakes as possible … or we can encourage the same attitude and same level of mistakes, but stress the importance of *improvement* over winning.

If we don't have in our coaches to foster healthy competition, we will make the easy decision and simply take away the scoreboard. Yet the best outcome would be to leave the scoreboard and have a coach who encourages mistakes, embraces learning opportunities, and helps kids to set goals. Simply put, we can take the easy way out and live in a nanny state, or we can teach and trust coaches to do the right thing.

It all comes down to having a great coach which unfortunately in this country there aren't enough of.

You can have it all—a coach and parent who are outcome-focused *and* encourage risk-taking. These things do not need to be mutually exclusive. It just takes good coaching and good parenting to see past winning and losing.

At AFLW; elite women's football; the focus on winning is intense. Yet despite the national focus on the game and results I still manage to have a mistakes-are-okay philosophy. If we can do it at AFLW level, then surely we can do it at an U/12 level.

At the Western Bulldogs AFLW where I am Head Coach, we talk a lot about vulnerability. My players are playing a game with the world's worst shaped ball, in little shorts and singlets, on the world's biggest oval in pouring rain and wind in front of a national TV audience. If you aren't prepared to be vulnerable and make mistakes, then you simply aren't going to be very good at the game.

The fact is over-competitiveness in kids' sports only exists when the people in charge (the adults) don't do the right thing. They don't let kids make mistakes because, to *them*, the result is too important.

So why should the kids miss out on important life lessons like those discussed above because adults can't help themselves? They shouldn't, but herein lies the dilemma.

If winning and competition is important to humanity and realising human potential, surely it is worth exploring. When it comes to kids' sports, the answer is no, not yet. In Chapter 3 we will explore the reasons why children aren't wired to concentrate heavily on winning.

Activity 1—Statements

In the meantime, here are some statements to ponder. Read each statement and then answer 'yes', 'no', or 'unsure'. Reflect closely on both yours and your child's behaviour in these situations.

Statements	Yes	No	Unsure
My child responds negatively to a competitive environment.			
I miss opportunities to teach and reinforce the positive lessons competition can bring.			
My child would say I am very competitive.			
There are elements of my behaviour that I am uncomfortable with.			
People have mentioned how competitive I am while I'm at my child's sport.			
Our team/child has a negative reputation for sportsmanship amongst peers and parents.			
I talk more about winning than about playing and having fun.			
I am unsure if my child's sport/ team environment offers a healthy level of competition.			

If you answered 'yes' to any of these questions, (note: it's not good to have 'yes' answers) consider the effects of this behaviour on your child. How do they react when you display the behaviours you list?

For example, when I talk about winning, does my child get fired up, or do they walk away or change the subject? Do I have to keep making my point because they aren't listening like I want them too?

If you do have a 'yes' answer ...

1. Make a list of the behaviours you want to eradicate.
2. Make a list of more appropriate behaviours you can deploy going forward.
3. Consider whether you need to talk to the coach about fostering a healthier environment.

For example:

- Behaviour to eradicate—I will not study the ladder each week and drum it into the kids. I will not tell them how important it is to win so we can move up one spot.
- More appropriate behaviour—I will find out what the kids are working on and encourage them to try it in the game, without focusing on the result.

If you answered 'unsure' to any question ...

1. Conduct some serious self-reflection.
2. Seek advice from friends, coaches and parents you trust to give you honest answers. Ask them, 'Do you think I am over-competitive?' And, if so, 'What actions tell you that?'
3. Think about the answers you get and decide if your behaviour is healthy or unhealthy.

The rest of Chapter 1 will be devoted to actions you can use to help realign your priorities.

Action 1—The totem pole effect and success criteria

Why you shouldn't place all your emphasis on wining, and what to do if you do.

It pays to understand that competition is a natural human instinct. Remember when our kids were smaller and we wanted them to go and get their pyjamas from their room. We would say, 'I will count to see how long it takes you.' The competitive juices; even for those as young as five years old; kicks in, and off they race up the hallway, hoping to get faster than last night's time. We didn't teach the kids how to do this, it just comes naturally. Although the pace *I* showed could have been to avoid getting caught by the monster that may or may not have lived under the stairs as I shot up to my second-floor bedroom.

The important thing is that at age five, losing is not devastating to a child's self-esteem. It is when children reach seven and eight years old that they start to realise that there are other people in this competition, and the concept of comparison kicks in. Some psychologists call it the 'totem pole effect' whereby, in kids' minds, they start to place the smart kids on top, along with the good-looking kids and the fast kids. It is at this age that kids start to understand that with every winner there is a loser. And if they are in the latter, it's possible that their confidence and self-esteem will take a hit. Essentially, *I'm not running for the pyjamas anymore just in case I* don't *get faster than last night, and you think I am a loser.*

Of course, no parent would ever think that, but remember we are dealing with young kids here.

And here is the killer punch—Nim Tottenham, Associate Professor of Psychology at Columbia University, says that the section of the brain that helps kids manage the big emotions of losing is the last to develop.[4] This means they need lots of help coping.

Simply, your child is not mentally equipped to cope with the pressure and emotions that a 'win at all costs' attitude places on their developing mind. By forcing your child to deal with emotions they are as yet ill-equipped to manage, you may be doing irreversible harm.

It's not just me saying this—it's the scientists. I do recognise that, though the phrase 'win at all costs' is used here, this mentality should never be adopted in kids' sports. Though, let's not mistake never winning at all costs for never winning *at all.*

So what do we do about our kids' fragile relationships with losing? How do we tread the fine line between having them compete and strive to win without inflicting psychological stress?

Though I don't agree with the modern theory that every kid should receive the same trophy at the end of the season, or that we should banish scoreboards from junior games in case some kids feel sad about losing ... I do think there is space between the 'win at all costs' and 'there are no losers' dichotomy.

This is the space that parents (and coaches) should operate. In other words, have a scoreboard, allow someone to be the winner, but *handle the situation appropriately.*

What can I focus on besides winning and losing?

One of the ways to do this is to understand what the success criteria is for your child and your child's team. If you are unsure what these are then sit down with your child's coach and ask the question, 'What is my child working on?' If the coach is any good, they will immediately be able to tell you. It should be things like 'striking of the ball', 'shooting from outside the key' or 'first touch with her left foot', et cetera. This will allow you to take your focus off of *winning* and concentrate on what your child is doing in the game.

It is impossible to win every time you play a game. No player in the history of sport has ever done that, so why should we expect our kids to be able to do it? It is far better to concentrate on our kids' improvement. To achieve this, we need to understand and look at the things they are working on. In this way, success does not relate solely to what the scoreboard says—rather, it relates to what your child does in the game. In essence you can 'win' even when you 'lose'.

Many parents only focus on the scoreboard because they don't know what else to focus on. If this is you, ask your kids what they are working on, learn how the game is played and maybe even get out and have a kick or hit yourself. You may just realise that the free throw line is further out than it looks from the sideline and you can cut your kid some slack when they miss one.

Or maybe next time you drop your kid off for golf lessons, grab a bag of balls and hit some yourself. I doubt every ball will go straight, and it may make you appreciate how hard the game is.

A useful exercise I always ask parents to do is sit and watch a professional game and see how many basic skill errors are made. You will need plenty of paper and a few pens as I guarantee the numbers will astound you. Sure the mistakes will often be overshadowed by glimpses of brilliance, but you'll realise that even professional basketballers miss layups, soccer players miss from dead in front, tennis players serve double faults and golfers hit it in the water (and so will your kids, who *aren't* professionals).

By placing more emphasis on improvement rather than winning you immediately lighten the load on your child.

And guess what—you can actually improve and win at the same time. These things are not mutually exclusive.

I become incredibly frustrated with coaches who cannot grasp this concept. They focus so heavily on skill development that they actively promote 'not winning' as a positive part of the game day. It's basically whoever can hang on to the ball the longest is the winner; forget about the posts with the net in between.

It staggers me how they are allowed to get away with this. As an example, they will promote 'keeping the ball' and demand that every pass has to go to a teammate's feet; even if this means passing to a teammate behind you or someone in a worse position; as long as your team keeps possession of the ball. I have seen junior teams at National Carnival level be fantastic at maintaining possession, but go nowhere near the goals. On every occasion they lost the game and we parents had to put our sports psych hats on and rebuild the confidence of kids who came with the hope of being competitive.

In my mind a far better option would be to teach the kids how to maintain possession as a means of *scoring*. Passing should be a means to an end (scoring), not simply a means of keeping possession. I understand there are game situations when you may need to simply maintain possession, but primarily the aim is to score.

Ideally the success criteria should be to maintain possession and work the ball into an area where you can score. If the team loses, then we can evaluate the game by how many times they passed the ball into a scoring position.

You can't do any of these things properly if you have eradicated all scoring—winning and losing—from the game.

If a goal isn't scored then that's okay, as long as they made progress on their success criteria. If they do happen to end up on the right side of the margin, then guess what? You will have some happy kids who will be eager to turn up to training again next week.

Either way they have something to be happy about.

In the worst-case scenario, they don't meet their success criteria *and* they don't win—well, that's when you need to be a great sports parent. First and foremost, understand that, as we mentioned previously, nobody wins every game they play. Check your level of perspective on the result and be the adult about it. Ask yourself what sort of mindset you want your child to have and foster that. Regardless of what your mindset is or how frustrated you are, your child's mindset is the only one that counts. In Chapter 5 we explain ten ways you can assist your child in times like these.

Most importantly, understanding the success criteria helps you with what to say when they come walking over with their little faces all upset. It will guide you on the all-important ride home in the car (often the most awkward time in the whole sports event).

If the kids know their success criteria, they will understand when you say to them, 'Hey, you guys were great at your passing today. You had the ball in your box about twenty times.' It will take the sting out of the scoreboard, which denotes them as the losers. It won't suddenly have them jumping for joy but it will help them keep perspective. And once they know that mum and dad aren't solely focused on the score then it's okay for them not to be either. The sooner they get into this mindset, the sooner and more eager they will be to get to practice and improve on their success criteria.

If they did manage to win, the conversation is, 'Great you won! It's because you have been working so hard on your passing and did it so well today.' Not because, 'You guys are better than the other team.'

Do you start to see how the success criteria links in with winning and losing? The focus is on the small aspects of the game; getting them right so that the outcome will be winning, not the other way around where the entire focus is on winning, no matter how it's achieved.

I have spoken to Olympic athletes who say that they focus on the outcome (winning and losing a medal) for about 20 percent of the time. The remaining 80 percent is what they have to do to achieve the outcome—the success criteria.

Here's a tip for coaches. If you want to keep parents off your back, then communicating success criteria is the way to go. At the start of the season get all the parents together and communicate the following points:

1. **This is the impact I am going to have on these kids, as defined by the following focus areas** (note these are just a range of examples; don't do all of them):
   - Fun—all the kids will love playing this sport.
   - Teamwork—I am going to teach them the importance and joy of being in a team.
   - Skills—I am going to work on their skills.
   - Fitness—I will prepare them for the next level (age appropriate).
   - Game plan—I will teach them the nuances of the sport.
   - Promotion—I will get this team to a higher level; competition.

2. **How I am going to achieve this impact:**
   - Fun—we will play games at training and have a few social events like 'pie nights'.
   - Teamwork—I will promote and reward the team players, not individual brilliance.
   - Skills—we will make lots of mistakes in games, but I want players trying new skills under pressure.
   - Fitness—I expect a high training attendance.
   - Game plan—we may lose games early, but I want to teach them the right way to play.
   - Promotion—I will have a high emphasis on winning and as such will play my best team.

3. **What I am going to use to measure this impact:**
   - Fun—survey the kids during and after the season plus training attendance.
   - Teamwork—Key Performance Indicators (KPIs) such as shepherds, assists, encouragement of others, et cetera.

- Skills—test the kids and retest during the year on key skill elements.
- Fitness—fitness tests plus the ability to run out a game.
- Game plan—KPIs will be introduced as well as video reviews each week.
- Promotion—the ladder and win loss ratios.

Here's the part where it helps: When a parent comes up to you and asks, 'Why aren't we focused on winning?', you can respond with: 'I told you at the start of the year we were going to focus on *fun* and *teamwork* this year. If you didn't like that, you had an opportunity to speak up then, or take your child to another team.'

Importantly, provide the parent with proof that the kids are enjoying themselves. For example, 'Our attendance at training has been 100 percent, plus the kids' surveys say they love coming to play footy and have all re-signed for next year.' Job done.

Without knowing your success criteria you have no comeback to the parent, and indeed the parent has the right to ask these questions. In the best-case scenario, other parents will cut off the unhappy parent before they get to you by reminding them of your pre-season message.

The questions above are also incredibly useful for parents who want to know what to ask when determining if this team is the right team for their child. You are well within your rights to ask, 'What impact are you going to have on my child?' If the coach can't answer then warning signs need to go up. If they answer with something you don't like then you can at least make a decision based on facts.

Oh, and just quickly—this newfangled Athlete Centred Development (ACD) approach to coaching isn't meant for kids. Basically ACD stipulates that athletes should take ownership of their careers by evaluating their abilities, setting their own goals and devising their own training plans. Coaches are simply a resource they can use to improve, but the onus is placed firmly on the athlete. This is great for adult athletes, but not for kids. Kids need guidance. They need to be told specifics otherwise they will simply tell the coach what they think he or she wants to hear.

Kids also have trouble remembering to pack a lunch for school every day, or where they left their shoes. Expecting them to have their eyes on long-term goals and the processes required to achieve those goals is unrealistic at best. A far better approach it is to work with the kids on one thing they are working on *right now*. One skill, one part of the game, and that's it.

It may mean improvement in their entire game is slower, but you are more likely to improve when you concentrate on one thing at a time rather than stuffing up ten things at once. If you have identified what your child is working on now, and if you really must analyse the game (you don't always have to, you know) then that is what you talk about both before and after the game—the discussion does not have to be solely about winning or losing.

Hopefully now you can see how understanding the success criteria for the team and your child can take pressure off of winning and losing without the need to do away with competition completely. To me, the ban on scoreboards is a complete overreaction and caters to the bad parents and coaches. A few bad eggs spoiling it for the rest of us.

In Chapter 4 we will look at how parents, through sport, can promote positive life skills that will stay with the child forever.

Action 2—Promote positive life skills

Positive life skills, enjoyment, perseverance, overcoming adversity, teamwork, understanding the value of practice—these are all qualities you can learn from sport and, importantly, are not dependent on winning. In fact you can learn more positive things from losing than you can from winning (but only if there *are* losers).

Obviously, I am not saying you should try to lose. I am saying that when you think of all the life lessons losing can teach, you will approach winning and losing with a different mindset.

Consider this: I was recently told about a friend's son's basketball team won every game for the season. The next season they were moved up a grade and approached the games chock-full of confidence. As it turned out their confidence was misguided, as the leap in standard was greater than they predicted. They lost every game and in turn the 'happiest team' in the stadium turned into the 'ugliest team' in the stadium. The level of aggression between parents escalated, relationships with the coach soured, and the players started to shirk off training commitments and were visibly not enjoying themselves. All of this was because a group of kids and parents didn't know how to lose. They had become so fixated with winning that they failed to see the lessons that can come with losing. Perhaps if they had have stopped and thought, *okay, what can the boys learn from this?*, they wouldn't have disintegrated so quickly.

They could have gotten together and said, 'Boys, instead of losing by twenty points as we have done in the first three games, how about we aim to be less than ten points down at half-time? And here is how we are going to do it.' And then compared the mood after the game if they still lost by twenty but were only six points down at half-time. What if some of the stuff they were learning at training was the reason why they were only six down at the half? What would that teach them?

And what about the boys who decide to give up the game completely because it was no longer as fun as it was when they were winning? What lessons would they learn about perseverance or resilience? If they left the game, the only lesson they would learn is that when things get a bit tough, it is okay to just turn your back and walk away.

None of these life lessons would be possible if the focus was solely on improving rather than winning. The scoreboard tells you how much improvement you have got to do, or how much your hard work is paying off—that's all.

If you need further proof that winning isn't everything, consider this:

In a July 2016 study published in the Journal of Physical Activity & Health, researchers interviewed children who played organised soccer and found that having fun was the primary reason for their participation. Other reasons included learning and improving, developing team friendships, and participating in team rituals.[5]

Winning ended up way down the list. Out of eighty-one determinants that make playing sports enjoyable, the children rated 'winning' forty-eighth, said Amanda Visek, lead author of the study and Associate Professor of Sports Psychology at George Washington University in Washington, D.C.

'While surprising, this is positive,' she said. 'Sports by definition includes competition, and the outcome of a competition results in winning and losing. But the findings from our study highlight that the fun experience is not determined by the end result of a game but rather by the process of physically engaging in the game.'[6]

It's an interesting finding to say the least and flies in the face of academics who say that sport must be fun, therefore we must eliminate all scoring, awards and recognition of achievements.

So what do we do? One theory espouses that the best way to handle winning and losing is to *not care*. Basically, go into the game with zero expectations or focus on the outcome. Whatever happens will happen. Whilst there is some merit in not caring too much, it begs the question: are we just avoiding the real issue? And when did avoidance become an acceptable way to deal with adversity?

A far better approach is to acknowledge the result, evaluate what you can learn from the result and move on. Having said that, you don't need to learn something from every game. Even at AFL level there were games that could be described as disastrous, and the best way to deal with them was to forget and move on immediately. For kids this should be the norm rather than the exception and for young kids especially; if they are okay with the result, then you have to move on, too.

We all know there isn't a manual that they hand out when you have kids. For many of us, we do our best with what we have, hopefully learning from role models that came before us and bits and pieces we pick up along the way. Our role is to raise good members of society who will have a positive influence on the people and environment around them. This involves teaching them skills that will enable them to navigate life's downs, and capitalise on life's ups. If we do that, then in my opinion it's a job well done.

It is far more important to produce a good person; a positive member of society; than a sporting champion. If you can manage both like a Mr and Mrs Federer can claim, then good on you. But remember, a good person is a successful person, so concentrate on that first and foremost.

Below is a chart that details some common life skills. It shouldn't take you long to see opportunities in your child's life where you can reinforce or teach these skills.

Life skills	Opportunities
Decision making	This includes in-game decisions plus determining inevitable sacrifices that need to be made in order to succeed. Don't forget choosing priorities, goals and the things they enjoy doing in life. For example, *do I go out with my mates or be fresh for training?*
Problem solving	Resist the temptation to give the kid every answer and solve every problem. Choose what you let them decide and be prepared—they may not always choose the response you would. For example, *how do I go about getting the position I want in the team?*
Creative/lateral thinking	Encourage them to think of alternate solutions; something different from what their friends would do. Use reasoning that isn't immediately obvious. For example, *I haven't beaten this person for a long time. What can I do differently?*
Critical thinking	Base decisions on clear evidence and research rather than gut decisions. For example, *I want to get faster, so I will research speed drills rather than just hope I'll get faster.*
Effective communication	Everyone learns to communicate, but can they communicate tough messages, their feelings, injustices, et cetera? Can they seek clarification when they are unsure? For example, *I don't get what the coach was talking about, so I will go and see her after training and ask her to explain it again.*
Interpersonal skills	Encourage strong, deep, close relationships even if they are short term. For example, *these girls in the team are different to me but I have found some common ground and we get along great now.*
Self-awareness	Understand who they are apart from a sportsperson, their environment, and other individuals. This prevents them from being caught in the cycle of good performance = good person; bad performance = bad person. For example, *that missed goal doesn't make me a bad person—just someone who may need a bit more practice.*

Life skills	**Opportunities**
Empathy	The ability to share and feel another person's emotions. This is an underrated component of sportsmanship and these days a requirement for effective leadership. For example, *realise when teammates go a bit quiet and, importantly, do something about it (like have a chat to see why).*
Assertiveness	Being self-assured and confident without being aggressive. This is an oft underrated skill that can be characterised as good old *standing up for yourself.* For example, *a young girl who refuses to play second fiddle to the boys in a mixed gender team.*
Coping mechanisms	Have techniques to solve interpersonal problems as well as master, minimise or tolerate stress and conflict. For example, *practice mindfulness so you can calm yourself during stressful times before and after games.*
Resilience	Successfully adapt to life tasks in the face of highly adverse condition. This will involve developing techniques and strategies to cope with the tough times. For example, *you don't quit when you don't make the A team.*

Now complete Activity 2 below: Choose a couple of life skills you think your child would do well to strengthen.

When you attend their games, look for opportunities to reinforce these skills. If this is your focus, the scoreboard will become irrelevant to you. Or in fact, it will become your biggest ally, offering you greater teaching opportunities. Learning generally comes from defeat, as success can often wallpaper over cracks.

Activity 2—Positive life skills

Life lessons to reinforce this season:

1. ______________________________

2. ______________________________

Tips:

- Base this on your expectation of the season. For example, is the team likely to win more than they lose, or lose more than they win? Your focus may then turn to teaching how to be gracious winners or resilient losers.
- Continually look out for sporting and non-sporting opportunities to reinforce the lessons.
- Never miss an opportunity to reinforce or reward the right behaviours. Don't simply be on the lookout for examples of poor behaviour. Use the carrot twenty times more than you use the stick.
- Stick to two life lessons and do them well because if you try to teach everything at once, you will more than likely stuff them all up. Do two, get them right, then move your focus to two more.

Action 3—No-one likes a sore loser

Growing up, I reckon my three sisters and I finished board games about 20 percent of the time. Often the game would end when one person (usually me) was exposed for cheating; or as soon as it was inevitable one of us would lose, the board would become airborne. To this day I don't know how a game of *Monopoly* ends.

Some would say we were competitive bunch, others a bunch of sore losers. Often it is a fine line between the two.

It's true that nobody likes a sore loser. So what do you do if your child's competitiveness boils over into sore loser territory?

Here's five things you should try:

1. **Praise effort, not outcome.**

   If a child thinks the only way that they will get a pat on the back is by winning, then that is what they will concentrate on. To them anything but a win will not be good enough. The pressure to always win builds and their under-developed brains will not be able to cope—resulting in unsociable behaviour.

   The fact is, nobody wins all the time. Teach your child that the effort they apply to the game is more important than winning. If they give their all and lose, then that's okay. It doesn't mean they are a failure; they just need to get better at what they do. Sore losers don't understand this—they are more likely to blame someone else for them losing and can't consider their own contribution towards the outcome.

2. **Don't 'let' them win.**

   As much as you think it is easier to let them win (in board games, darts, et cetera), it doesn't help them. It just reinforces that they always *need* to win. As a parent you don't have to be ultra-competitive; just don't throw the game to avoid a tantrum. It is far better to understand that sometimes you win and sometimes you lose—you have to learn how to deal with both. My kids know that I will never *allow* them to win at anything. Success must be earned, or it isn't a success.

3. **Show them how.**

   Regardless of the result, insist your child shows good grace after a game by shaking the opponent's hand and saying 'well done' to the ref. Quite often the child becomes a sore loser because you have opened the door to allowing the bad behaviour. Did you give in when they threw a tantrum, or did you refuse to take them to McDonalds after they stormed off the field? You get what you settle for, so think about the bad behaviour you have settled for in the past and agree not to tolerate it anymore. Role-modelling good behaviour is one of the most important jobs you have.

4. **Teach your child about feelings.**

   Help your child recognise when they are sad, angry, frustrated, disappointed, et cetera. Talk about how they are feeling after a game, not just about the game itself. Recognising when and why they are frustrated helps the child deal with the emotions they are feeling. Combine this with coping strategies like deep breathing, removing themselves from the situation or verbalising that they are frustrated. This will help prevent the uncontrolled behaviour that sore losers exhibit. Invest time and energy into teaching your child specific anger management skills that will help them tolerate losing.

5. **Remind them why they play.**

   Winning should never be the sole measure of success for kids. Playing sport at a junior level should be more about fun, improvement, friends and activity than it is about winning. Make sure your child recognises this. Your first question should always be, 'Did you have fun today?' Sore losers lose perspective and see only winning and losing as a measurement. Remind the kids of the other fun things besides winning. Point out small things they did in the game so they know that they don't have to win in order to receive praise from you or to be seen as a good person.

Now, all of this doesn't mean you have to be happy with losing. There aren't many champions who are happy about losing. Playing to win is an important part of sports and indeed life. Again, the key is keeping everything in perspective.

Without perspective a sore loser is unable to properly assess *why* they lost or figure out what they *need to do* to avoid losing again. This ability to reflect upon an event and make changes is vital.

It's what good losers do. It's what champions do.

Chapter 1—Summary

Winning is part of sports, and it is part of life. Despite varied opinions on the subject, becoming a winner may be one of the most important things a person can do in their lifetime. If we devalue winning in our lives, then we can say goodbye to an enormous amount of untapped human talent and capacity that will never surface to benefit humanity or enable people to experience being the best that they can be.

Competition has many benefits, including …

- Competition teaches us to bring our best effort.
- Competition teaches us to manage our nerves.
- Competition teaches us to cope when things do not go our way.
- Competition helps us with goal-setting.
- Competition teaches us to play by rules.
- Competition helps us to learn to win and lose with grace.
- Competition is fun.
- Competition can build self-esteem.
- Competition teaches commitment.
- Competition gives us another community.

The totem pole effect

When children reach seven to eight years old, they start to realise that competition is not just about themselves, and *comparison* starts to kick in. It is at this age that kids start to understand that with every winner there is a loser. And if they are in the latter, it's possible that their confidence and self-esteem will take a hit.

There is an ideal space between the 'win at all costs' and 'there are no losers' dichotomy.

Avoiding the 'win at all costs' mentality

Concentrate on success criteria

It is impossible to win every time you play a game. No player in the history of sport has ever done that, so why should we expect our kids to be able to do it? It is far better to concentrate on our kids' improvement. To achieve this, we need to understand and look at the things they are working on.

You can actually improve and win at the same time. These things are not mutually exclusive.

Concentrate on building positive life skills

Positive life skills, enjoyment, perseverance, overcoming adversity, teamwork, understanding the value of practice—these are all qualities you can learn from sport and, importantly, are not dependent on winning.

The scoreboard tells you how much improvement you have got to do, or how much your hard work is paying off.

Teach your child how to be a good loser

- Praise effort.
- Don't *let* them win.
- Show them how.
- Teach them about feelings.
- Remind them why they play.

Chapter 2

Issue: You place undue pressure on your child

This is the area that truly defines a sports parent with an issue: a person who cannot separate sporting performance from their affections towards their children. This is also the area that most parents are in denial over.

Naturally, you say that you love your child no matter what, and I have no doubt that you do. But ask yourself this simple question:

Is the ride home frosty after a poor game and joyful when they play well?

If this is you, then you may have an issue.

By this, I am not talking about the monster parent who home-schools his kid just so he can make sure they are practicing eight hours a day and not wasting time with friends (or, as he will term them, 'bad influences'). Tennis seems to have a lot of these types of parents for some reason. Recent revelations by Jelena Dokic highlights how prevalent and damaging these types of parents are. Unfortunately they are not confined to tennis—pretty much every sport where a decent dollar can be earned has their fair share of parents with issues. These parents need far more intervention than simply reading this book.

I am more so talking about the parents who want to do the right thing by their kids, or think they are doing the right thing by their kids but are unsure of what the 'right thing' actually is. And in their confusion, they might exhibit behaviours that are potentially damaging to their kids.

Quite often the causes of this type of behaviour include parents experiencing athletic competition for the first time, whilst others believe their child represents a second chance at righting the wrongs of their not-so illustrious athletic past. The child's success gives them a chance to bask in the reflected glory of their children, or dispel some of the feelings of regret and disappointment that they couldn't achieve these same goals. These feelings, if strong enough, can impair rational thoughts and potentially lead to the types of behaviour outlined in Activity 3 below.

Studies have shown that parents who can clearly identify a failed goal; such as never achieving tennis stardom, never learning to play an instrument, or failing to write a novel; are more likely to place higher demands on their children to achieve these things. The real danger in these circumstances is that their children will struggle to establish their own identity and see themselves as existing simply to please other people.

Can you imagine the stress it places on a child if they notice that you appear to love them more when they win than when they are losing to a better team or person? Not only do they have to contend with losing, but also the fact that the most important person in their life now thinks less of them. How devastating is that for a child?

But would you tell your child that if they lose a game, you would love them a bit less? No, you wouldn't. So why do you send obvious signals, such as cold shoulders and passionless hugs that communicate exactly the same thing as those hurtful words? Why do you stand there with a sour look on your face after seeing a mistake? Why do you talk about how much *you* and the rest of the family are sacrificing for *their* sport? Do you play the martyr card in front of other parents?

Kids are very perceptive when it comes to their mum's and dad's feelings, so don't for one minute think that they haven't noticed. Even the most unobservant kid can still pick up when mum or dad isn't happy with them. Think of the pressure placed on developing sports kids when they think they have to please their coach, their teammates, win the game, not look silly, avoid mistakes, look tough, and *not* be a disappointment to their parents.

It would be debilitating.

You may say your kid doesn't feel this way, but do you know for sure?

Effects of pressure

The effects of this kind of pressure can be devastating. Instead of enjoying rides to practices and games or running drills with you in the back yard, the child may avoid the sport and, worse still, *you* altogether.

In the end, this lack of connection with you may cause the child to stop voicing their needs. Lines of communication between parent and child must remain open to ensure that you have the chance to assist with the many stresses your child with inevitably go through. If your child cannot talk openly with you, they may keep their feelings bottled up or become emotionally dependent on peers (who may not have the experience to handle the issue or have your child's best interests at heart). Having a child who openly and freely communicates with you is deeply valuable.

And then, of course, there is the growing issue of cyber and face-to-face bullying. Having a child who can openly discuss concerns and incidents with you is one of the most important prevention strategies a parent can employ against bullying. If your child can't talk about sport with you for fear of an adverse reaction, how will they approach the subject of an inappropriate schoolyard or social media interaction? It is likely they won't, which is why the old 'my door is always open' scenario isn't good enough. You have to prove time and time again that it is okay for them to *walk through* the door. Sport is a great way to establish that communication with your child, but it won't happen if they think that you are an overly judgmental parent.

There are many stories of champion junior athletes who gave up competing way too early because they couldn't cope with emotional pressure from their parents. And there are a thousand more stories of people you have never heard of that quit before they became famous. In fact, a National Alliance for Youth Sports poll in the US that states that 70 percent of kids drop out of sport by the time they are thirteen.[7]

Dropping out

It's important to note that dropping out of a sport should not be seen as the catastrophe some of us believe. Those of us with late-teen kids can look back at all the things they tried over the years, but never maintained. My own girls have never been seen as quitters but at one time or another have all undertaken dancing lessons, music lessons, drama lessons, art lessons, played basketball, tennis, touch rugby, karate, milo cricket … and have quit all of them! They all settled on soccer or AFL as their sport of choice, which makes one thing out of ten that they have struck with.

My point is that *kids will quit*. It's what they do. And we actually encourage it when we say, 'Try all the different sports and then settle on the one you love.' I'm sure we have all given that advice at one point or another. So, quitting and trying something else they may love is really just them following our advice.

Not playing a sport should not be seen as the end of the world. Sure, there are the health and social benefits that accompany playing sport and I could cite numerous studies which say that a lifelong love of sport is helpful—but it isn't the end of the world. Maintaining a healthy lifestyle is the key. It doesn't matter how they do it. If it turns out to be kickboxing classes at the gym that they enjoy, then great—they are keeping fit and having fun. What more can you want?

Or is the problem that *you* want more?

The most important point to consider here is this: If your child chooses not to play sport, it must be because *they* have made that choice, and not because they have been driven away from sport by your actions. I say again—*not by your actions.*

To prevent this scenario from occurring, work your way through the following activity. It will give you strategies to ensure you don't become one of those parents.

Activity 3—Self-assessment

Try answering the following questions honestly. The questions refer to how you react and treat your child before and after competition.

Question	Yes	No
Do they get hugs when they win and the cold shoulder when they don't?		
Do you wait outside the change rooms when they win, and in the car with the motor running when they lose?		
Do you ever talk to other parents and say how hopeless your child was today?		
Are your hugs less affectionate, or your 'good night' just a mumble when they lose?		
Are post-game treats only after wins?		
Is your encouragement louder when they are playing well and silent when they aren't?		
Does your child shy away from you after a loss or a poor game?		
Do you only post on social media to commemorate wins or good performances, and never just to highlight the fun that you and your child are having?		

If you answered 'yes' to any of the above questions, then you may have an issue. It doesn't mean you are a bad parent—it means you have some work to do.

Move on to the next section and we will give an action to remedy your issue.

Action 1—The importance of self-reflection

The best treatment here is a thorough and honest session of self-reflection. Assess your thoughts on your child when they win and when they lose. Be honest—does it change? Are you more inclined to be short-tempered with them when they don't do well, even just a little bit?

If so, then you need to change quickly. This is a sure-fire way to drive a wedge between you and your child. Your love for them should not be dependent on how they perform on a sporting field (or in the classroom, for that matter).

The key here is to be in control of your feelings, not reacting to the situation but choosing how to act.

I am going to assume that you do not want your child thinking your love for them is dependent on their performance. If you do, then stop reading—you are beyond help. If you don't, then you need to exercise some self-control. Simply saying to yourself, 'I will never, ever get down or disappointed again' is unsustainable.

Good intentions don't mean much here; it's all about actions. In my book, intentions are useless. Nothing changes when you *intend* to do something. Only when you *act* will things change. Remember, your car doesn't keep going because you *intend* to petrol in it. It keeps going because you act—you fill it up! The same theory applies here. What are you going to *do* differently is the question.

Chances are you will find yourself upset at times, even disappointed. The key is, while you are learning not to feel this way, to maintain control of your actions. As mentioned above, this involves choosing your actions carefully.

Eliminate actions that outwardly show your child that you are displeased with them. The cold shoulders, the stern looks, the feeble hugs. Choose to replace them with warm hugs, sincere smiles and non-sport conversations. Basically you are being an adult and controlling your attitude—the way you think feel and act—rather than letting things outside of your control determine your attitude for you. Sounds easy, doesn't it? Well, it isn't.

Your attitude and you

For most of our lives we have allowed events outside of our control to dictate our attitudes. For instance, do you get out of bed on rainy mornings and instantly think *today is going to be a crappy day*? Unless you have the power to change the weather, why would you let something outside of your control determine your attitude? It doesn't make sense.

Do you get home from work and stew over the one bad thing that happened in a day of ten other good things? This, too, doesn't make sense.

Does the person who doesn't drive the second the traffic light turns green force you to angrily jump on the horn as if wasting two seconds will ruin your entire day? Again, it doesn't make any sense—especially considering the ability to choose how you think, feel and act is the most powerful asset you have.

Imagine if someone said to you that you must think this particular way or you must feel this particular way. You would be up in arms. Yet we give that power to other people all the time: 'I feel angry because of what some other person in a car did.' But you don't even know that person, so why would you give them the power to make you feel angry? My kid's team lost a game—I wasn't out on the field, I didn't play, but I am still angry about it.

It doesn't make sense.

The great Victor Frankl, eminent psychologist and Holocaust survivor, once wrote, 'The last of the human freedoms: to choose one's attitude in any given set of circumstances, to choose one's own way.'[8]

Despite losing numerous family members to the atrocities of the concentration camps in World War Two, Victor believed that; no matter how horrendous and degrading the circumstances were; no-one could take away his ability to choose his own attitude.

Certainly puts into perspective any thoughts you may have that it is hard to choose your attitude (the way you think, feel and act) after a game of junior sport.

Victor also states that, 'Between stimulus and response there is a space. In that space is our power to choose our response. In that response lies our growth and our freedom.'[9]

In diagram form, it can be laid out like this:

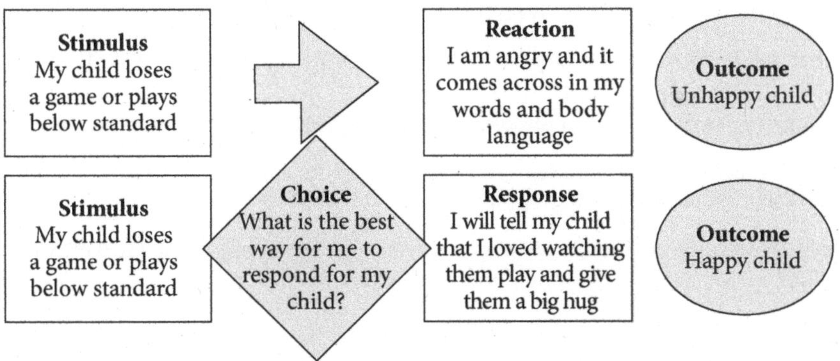

You may say that all of this is all well and good, but what about when my child gives a sub-standard effort in big games or lets the team down? Even in kids' sports there are big games, such as finals or playoffs, and it is hard not be disappointed in your child if they do not show the required effort. Especially when they reach youth level around fourteen years of age.

Effort and results

I have always told my kids that they can't control the outcome, but they can control their effort. There were times where I have been unhappy with how I handled this doctrine after games. As I mentioned earlier, I am naturally competitive person. I have no doubt there were times when I blurred the line between being unhappy about the result and being unhappy with my kids' effort. I think my kids linked the two and concluded that their lack of effort caused the loss of the game.

Looking back, I realise I handled these situations badly. They construed my negative demeanour to be a reflection on how their effort caused the defeat. I recall the extra effort required to get them enthused for training and games in the following weeks. How they just didn't seem to want to talk about any sport, not just their sport, for a while.

It is obvious now that I was the reason why their enthusiasm dropped. It's not something I am proud of and, and though I do believe I was well-intentioned, intention means very little when you hurt your kids.

I make this point to emphasise that nobody is perfect. If you read this book without making any links back to your own behaviour then you are either a saint or in denial. We all make mistakes; it's important to acknowledge them and then find solutions so as not to repeat them. I also realised that I rarely mentioned their effort when they won a game—only when they lost. Another bad sports parenting issue on my behalf! Effort is effort and should not just be a factor when they lose.

But effort is important … right?

In a team sport, giving a substandard effort is unacceptable. I agree; if you are part of the team in a competitive sport then you should, on all occasions (unless injury prevents), give your best effort. If you are mucking around with friends, then by all means fart about to your hearts content. As a coach and parent they may need you to differentiate between the two game types as some kids won't naturally know when to switch on their competitive spirits and when to pick and choose their effort levels.

However, it is vitally important that your kid never thinks that they are responsible for the entire team's outcome. Even if they are the best player in the team, they cannot be made to feel like the weight of the team rests on their shoulders.

It is, however, acceptable to have a level of expectation regarding the effort your child displays. To get your point across you may even use disappointment as a tool. The point is you must *choose* to be disappointed in a controlled manner, and for a controlled period of time. Never, ever lose control.

Growing up, the thought of disappointing my parents was more of an incentive to make good decisions than any corporal punishment they could dish out.

The key when it comes to sport is not to show the child that *you* are disappointed in them or make them feel that they have let *you* down. Remember it is not about you and they don't play for you! They play for themselves and the team, so it is okay to point out that how their lack of effort might have affected those two things—them, and the team. Reiterate that they are playing a team sport and part of the responsibility of playing a team sport is that they give of themselves to the team. This means trying as hard as they can, at all times.

The disappointment you have is in respect to your child not fulfilling their role in the team, or; for individual sports; not representing themselves in the best manner they can. Never, ever should it be about you, the parent, and whether or not they let *you* down.

That said, you are the parent, so it is still your job to teach them right from wrong.

Find out why

If your child's effort varies then the best course of action is to find out why this is happening. It is far healthier and longer-lasting to ask your child questions about what they are thinking and feeling and then getting to the bottom of the issue, rather than using guilt as a driver.

There may be a myriad of reasons for a substandard performance.

Your child may be having issues with other members of the team. They may be injured. They may be tired, or they may be just going through a growth phase and have no energy. Did your child skip breakfast this morning, or are they having trouble sleeping?

As a parent you need to know your child well enough to ask these questions and make these judgments. The solution to their lack of effort may be making sure they get to bed earlier the two nights before a game, instead of simply burdening them with your disappointment. Wouldn't that make for a far better drive home; rather than sitting in silence with your kid sulking in the back seat and you brooding in the front?

Understanding your child will stop the two of you from getting to the point where your love for them is even in question. It will also keep you rational and more able to see signs for why their effort was not as high as usual. If you are acting irrationally, you won't find the underlying issues that are driving their behaviour. And if *you* don't notice them, your child is highly unlikely to be forthcoming with them.

Post-game conversation

After the game, no matter how they played, the best thing you can do for your child is say, 'I love watching you play' or ask the question, 'Did you have fun?' If the answer is yes, then move on. If it's no, you need to ask questions. Don't drill them for answers; wait until the mood has increased and then broach the subject. Typically kids will stew for thirty minutes at most after a game before they are open to discussing events. Wait it out and then approach the subject from a caring perspective—not a judgmental perspective: 'You said you didn't have fun today, what was different today than last week when you were on a high?' Or, 'You didn't seem to have the same energy as last week, are you feeling okay?'

Get them to compare the two weeks, as this will prevent the likelihood of 'nothing' being the dismissive response.

If effort is the issue then be observant enough to calmly give them examples such as, 'You usually push forward into your forward area a little more than you did today.' Or, 'You seemed a bit more puffed than usual.' It may just be that the coach asked them not to push forward today or that it was hotter than it seemed—problem solved.

It may take several goes before you get a response. You will need to be diligent, especially if it looks like they aren't having fun. The most important thing you have to rule out is they think they are letting you down.

So, the answer is to always be in control of your emotions. Understand when you are acting adversely and ask yourself, *what message am I sending to my child by acting this way*? If it is anything other than a message that says *I love you and want the best for you*, then step away, compose yourself and return a good parent. Remember here that your job is not to be the coach, but to find solutions as to why your child didn't enjoy themselves.

Complete the activity below, as this may give you an insight into your child's current mindset.

Activity 4—Better choices

Make a list of the verbal and body language you will *choose* to adopt instead of reacting on your initial feelings:

1. ______________________________

2. ______________________________

3. ______________________________

Examples:

- After every game I will greet my child with a smile—no matter the result.
- During the game I will not show displeasure with my body language.
- In the car ride home I will wait not sit in silence, brooding over the result.

Activity 5—Warning signs for 'burnout'

Kids' bodies are not yet strong enough to cope with excessive physical or mental demands. At elite AFL levels, every action a player does during the week and game day is monitored to avoid burnout or injury. This is done for extremely hardy, seasoned playes, yet for kids we just keep wheeling them out.

If your child's effort or enthusiasm seems to be waning, you need to look for the signs. See the list below to determine if any apply to your child.

Signs of burnout—why your child may not be giving 100 percent effort

Tick possible reasons.

Sign	Y/N	Sign	Y/N
Increased levels of tension.		Increase in basic illnesses—coughs, colds, et cetera.	
Increased fatigue.		Inconsistent performance.	
Increased irritability/anger.		Depression.	
Decreased energy.		Feelings of inadequacy or insignificance.	
Decreased sleep.		Increased disappointment.	

If you responded 'yes' to any of the above, it may not mean simply stopping all activity. Here are some other actions you can consider.

- Take time off.
- Learn relaxation techniques.
- Introduce fun activities.
- Assess teammate interactions for issues.
- Assess coach interactions for issues.
- Reduce pressure to perform or attain high results.
- Determine if they are undergoing a growth spurt.
- Seek medical advice for physical or mental health concerns.
- Reduce the sport to its simple components—don't overcomplicate things.
- Lighten the training load for a period of time.
- Introduce other hobbies to take mind off sport for periods of time.

Note: Periods of rest are required for young bodies to grow. The energy saved when not training is converted into 'growing energy'. Try measuring your child at the start and end of the 'off-season' period and note the changes. You may be amazed at how the body uses the energy usually spent running around the court or pitch.

Ask your physio or sports doctor about how much rest and recovery each age group requires. Doing nothing may be the best thing you can have your child do.

Action 2—But my kids just aren't motivated!

Do you ever look at other people's kids and say, 'I wish mine were like them'? Or, 'Why is it that some kids just seem to be motivated, skilled and have the right attitude when mine are just lazy?'

If this is you, it doesn't mean you love them any less—it's just that you may have some late bloomers.

The fact is, most kids are motivated, just not necessarily motivated by the things that motivate *you*. Maybe homework doesn't motivate them, but playing sports or video games does.

The good news is the old saying 'they will grow out of it' may be true.

The prefrontal cortex, which is the 'executive centre' of the brain and responsible for emotions, attention span, perseverance and flexibility, develops at different rates. Sometimes it isn't until late adolescence before it kicks into gear and doesn't fully develop until the age of twenty-five.

The question is, what can parents do to avoid going mad while we wait for their brains to develop?

Here are my top five tips for managing unmotivated kids.

Look at the whole kid. By this, I mean don't get hung up on school grades or sports performance. What are they like with their friends, their family, or their peers? Are they a good, friendly person who relates well with others, has a social conscience, and obeys the rules? If they are, then these are often greater predictors of future success than grades on a test. Understand who your kid is on all levels, and all the roles they play in life, and you will probably find things that make you proud. They'll appreciate it when you notice.

The power of 'when you'. When you become an adult, it becomes clear that you get things only 'when you …' For example, you get paid 'when you' work; you get fitter 'when you' exercise; and you get more friends 'when you' are friendlier. Help your kid learn this by using 'when you' to good effect: You get dessert 'when you' eat your dinner; you get to play videos 'when you' finish homework; you get to play in a game 'when you' go to training. This helps kids learn structure and consequences even before they are consciously able to grasp it by themselves. Some psychologists say kids can't learn this concept until they turn twelve. I believe if we can teach a dog to sit up for a treat, we can teach a kid that the ice cream doesn't come until the carrots are gone.

Motivation or anxiety. What you see as lack of motivation and classify as laziness is often anxiety about not doing well. We adults avoid doing things that make us anxious and kids are no different. Understand what is going on in your kid's mind and create actual solutions to help. Just saying, 'Don't worry, you'll eventually get how to do trigonometry' won't help the anxiety, but hiring a tutor or asking the school for help—actually finding a solution—*will* help the anxiety. It will also relieve the perceived lack of motivation to study. Remember it is *actions* that will assist in these circumstances, not words alone.

Create good habits. For example, teach them how to study properly and remove distractions that prevent them from concentrating. Understand that their little brains are prone to distractions, so remove those as much as you can. Also utilise the school to find out what they are telling your child so you can be on the same page. Consistent messaging will eventually sink in.

Ask 'how', not 'why'. Avoid asking 'why' questions, like, 'Why did you leave your lunchbox at school?' Straight away, the child thinks they have to come up with a good excuse and will start to blame someone else or justify their actions. It will be the teacher's fault for ringing the bell early, or the rain's fault as they had to hurry inside. Instead, ask 'how' questions, such as, 'Okay, we agree leaving your lunchbox at school was not good ... how are you going to organise to get it back?' The child has to put their mind into solution mode, not excuse mode. Hopefully they will say something like, 'Tomorrow, take me to school early so I can look on the oval and in the lost property box. I will be able to search for it and still get to class on time.' This is a far more productive conversation than simply figuring out *why* it was left behind.

Importantly, concentrate on the now—not the future. Understand that your child hasn't reached their peak yet and will not be perfect. Be careful of constantly driving them forward.

Right now is the most important time for you to be involved in your kid's life. Concentrate on that; not on what they are going to do as adults (when they are no longer your responsibility).

Chapter 2—Summary

Putting undue pressure on your kids is an issue that truly defines an over-involved parent—a parent who cannot separate their affections from their child's sporting performance This is also the area that most parents are in denial over.

Studies have shown that parents who can clearly identify a failed goal are more likely to place higher demands on their children to achieve these goals in their stead. The danger here is that children fail to establish their own identity and see themselves as existing just to please other people.

Instead of enjoying rides to practices and games, or practicing drills with you in the back yard, the child may avoid the sport (and you!) altogether. Lines of communication between parent and child must remain open to ensure that you have the chance to assist with the many stresses your child with inevitably go through. If your child cannot talk openly with you, they may keep their feelings bottled up or become emotionally dependent on peers.

The key is to be in control of your feelings; not *reacting* to the situation but *choosing how* to act.

Chances are you will find yourself feeling disappointed at times in your child's effort. While you are learning not to feel this way, you have to learn how to control your actions and emotions.

Remember that your child doesn't play *for you*. They play for themselves and the team.

Reiterate to them that they are playing a team sport and part of the responsibility of playing a team sport is that they give of themselves to the team. This means trying as hard as they can.

The disappointment you feel should only be in respect to your child not fulfilling their role on the team, or—for individual sports—not representing themselves in the best manner they can.

After the game, no matter how they played, the best thing you can do for your child is say, 'I love watching you play', or ask the question, 'Did you have fun?'

Monitor your child for signs of burnout and act on the cautious side. Reduced effort may be a symptom of more than just a lack of caring.

Ways to motivate your kids:

1. Look at the whole kid.
2. The power of 'when you'.
3. Motivation and anxiety.
4. Create good habits.
5. Ask the right questions that result in solutions, not excuses.

Chapter 3
Issue: It's more about you than the kids

Do you move away from other parents when your kid makes a mistake? Are you friendlier to them when your kid is doing well? Are the Facebook posts to let people know what your kid is up to, or to brag about them? Is the thought of missing a game as bad as having a limb amputated?

If so, you may have an issue.

You may think this is extreme, but I have seen parents who refused to attend post-game get-togethers because their daughter had a bad day on the soccer pitch. The worst parents of all are the ones who are dancing around the sidelines when their child is having a blinder. They are the life of the party—high-fiving the team as they come off the ground and chatting to the coach afterwards. But when their child has a stinker, they are nowhere to be seen. Poor little Johnny walks out of the change room, scans the crowd looking for his mum and dad, only to be told by another parent that they are waiting for him in the car.

Sounds extreme, doesn't it? But I am sure you have all seen it—and maybe even done it.

In my own parenting career I have dealt with the fact that my kids come under extra scrutiny because they have a father who was a professional football player. The kids didn't know this but deep down I especially liked it when they played well. I knew that because of their surname they would be judged more severely than their teammates. It would either be *Nathan Burke's kids are good,* or *Nathan Burke's kids are no good* … no middle ground.

I'm not sure when it hit me how stupid this was. But I had an epiphany at some stage and decided the onlookers' opinions counted for absolutely nothing. If the kids did stink but had fun, then that was all that mattered. It was about the kids playing, not me. I suppose I may have just grown up and matured a bit, but whatever the reason, watching them play became far more enjoyable for everyone involved.

Other extreme cases I have personally witnessed include parents who un-tag themselves from Facebook posts because their kid's team lost and they don't want their friends to find out. I have even witnessed parents sit and cry in their cars after a twelve-year-old girl missed a penalty on the soccer pitch.

What were they afraid of—the other parents shunning them because of a mistake their child made? The answer is, amazingly, *yes*. Yes, they were, and it is incredibly sad that these parents could not separate the performance of their daughter from their own self-worth. And it is also incredibly sad that some parent groups think it's okay to ostracise a parent because of their child's performance. Unbelievably, I have witnessed this happen also. The parents of the talented kids get together in little groups while the parents of the less talented are excluded. Parent cliques can be just as damaging to youth sport as any coach or administrator. It happens too often, and it is disgraceful.

Self-esteem

However, before we touch on you, pesky parents, let's look at the importance of self-esteem amongst our kids. We can't deny that a young athlete's rate of learning and level of performance can be directly correlated to the way they feel about themselves. If they are feeling good, then they are more likely to play well. The same goes for when they are at school.

We had to learn this lesson at St Kilda FC when we drafted a few younger players who were quite frankly of a different generation to us older fellas. We would often ridicule them for their need to have a last-minute stop by the mirror on the way up the race and onto the ground. We couldn't understand the need to make sure their hair was in the right place when you are just about to go out and play a game of football in the rain and mud.

But then a more learned person pointed out that if the player liked what they saw in the mirror, they would most likely be in a better, more positive frame of mind to go out and play well. Each to their own, as they say. Personally, if I was concerned with how I looked I would have made sure I never put the helmet on and mouth guard in when in front of the mirror. Neither could be considered a fashion statement.

But back to your kids.

Kids and self-esteem

Self-esteem is a very important factor in not just kids' sporting lives but in their general lives as well. Quite simply, self-esteem is how you think about yourself. When you are confident in your abilities you tend to feel good about yourself, but when you are full of doubt and confusion then your self-esteem drops.

Self-esteem matters because it directly impacts the way children act every day. Your child's self-esteem affects their friendships with other children, their success in school, their ability to deal with problems and their overall confidence. Kids with healthy self-esteem are better equipped to deal with peer pressure and responsibility than kids who feel bad about themselves. Children with good self-esteem are also better able to deal with strong emotions, both good and bad, and to cope with challenges and frustrations when they arise.

There are some things you can do as a parent to ensure you give them every chance to have a strong and appropriate level of self-esteem.

Don't assume. One of the biggest issues with coaches and parents is that they assume the child knows what they are thinking. If a coach changes a player's position or starts them on the bench for a game, and doesn't tell them the reason why, the player will assume the worst. It's human nature to do so. They will assume that they are no longer performing well in that position or that the coach is unhappy with them, which is why she started them on the bench. In fact the real reason for the change could be that the coach already knows they can play in that position and therefore wants to see how they go in another position. Or maybe they are playing a weaker team, so why not start on the bench and give some other kids a bit of extra playing time?

Kids rarely have the perception abilities or wisdom to understand why a coach or parent makes decisions, so you need to tell them. If you don't, their little minds will wander off in all directions and possible destroy their self-esteem. Make sure you tell kids the whole story—don't allow their little minds to wander off.

Treat them with respect. Nobody likes to be disrespected and if you want respect, then treat others with respect. The kids will give their all for a coach who doesn't demean them in front of others and does the small things like listening to and valuing their opinions. Humiliation and fear will drive kids away from their sports, and from who knows what else. Unfortunately some parents feel it is okay to humiliate their own kids in front of others … mainly because they can. *They are my kids so I can say what I want*, often to get a laugh from other parents. For instance, 'You had a stinker today, son. Couldn't hit the side of a barn with your first serve.' It may be seen as a funny comment to others but the message to your child is one of disrespect.

Avoid comparisons. Nobody, whether you are an adult or child, likes being compared unfavourably to another person. If you have to compare, make it about a skill, such as, 'See how Josh bends his elbow on a serve? Try to see if you can copy that action.' Don't say, 'Josh is a much better server than you.' When the concept of comparison with other kids kicks in, it can kick in very strongly and easily get out of control. Don't feed the paranoia by constantly making comparisons between your kid and other kids. Especially teenage kids, where the Relative Age Effect (RAE) can be instrumental. The RAE refers to the differences in children seemingly of the same age because they play in the same team. However, a child born in January could be in a vastly different growth phase than a child born in November of the same year. Comparisons between these kids can be highly damaging to their psyche as the comparison would be highly unfair.

Girls in particular hate being compared to other girls. Often, I have had two of my daughters play in the same team and one idiotic coach decide to pit them against each other for a position. All that did was make the one who got the position feel bad because her sister didn't. Neither player can prosper in these conditions.

It's okay to challenge. Show your child that you believe in them and that they can get to the next level. If done correctly it can build self-esteem, as who doesn't like someone important—someone they respect—having faith in them? If you have a good relationship and are honest—for example, you don't give over-the-top praise when it is undeserved—the child will derive confidence from your confidence. Appropriate praise is the key here. This will earn you respect and credence when it comes time to say, 'You know what, you can compete with these girls.'

See problems as a chance to improve. Many parents and coaches want to ignore personal problems when it is time for sport. They will say, 'Don't bring that stuff to training, leave the personal problems at home.' A better way to look at it is to see these problems as chance to get to know the athlete or child better. Find out what makes them tick and you will be a far better coach or parent; able to do all the small things that help imporve the way players feels about themselves. Kids don't have the ability to compartmentalise their lives like we ask adults to do. They haven't worked out who they are and what roles they play in life, so everything tends to be mixed up in one complicated beast. If they are having trouble at school, it will translate onto the pitch or court and vice versa. If you are in a position of authority and can help the child, then it is incumbent on you to do so.

Don't equate self-esteem with performance. Don't play the 'you let me down' card or link performance to them as people. If a child knows that you will think less of them after a loss, they will run away from that sport the first chance they get and may even run away from you. If it is a team sport, don't individualise, because it is the team that loses—not one person. You can individualise if a player does something above and beyond their normal abilities or contributes to the team in a special manner, but never single out poor performers in public. Find a quiet, isolated moment to have a private chat about the game with the child—but again, never in front of others. Sensitive kids will catch on to their mates being singled out and could even have their own issues because of it. The quickest way to destroy self-esteem is to publicly humiliate a person.

Last but not least is the need to **role-model good behaviour**, and you can't do that if you have issues with your own self-esteem.

The coming pages will help you address your own self-esteem issues. But before then, take a minute to evaluate the self-esteem of your child.

Activity 6—Self-esteem

The following are signs of healthy self-esteem.

Firstly, answer the questions from *your* perspective, and then answer them again—this time from how you think *your child* would answer the questions. Try to be realistic—even if you have an upbeat child, they won't always believe the best in themselves.

Feeling	**Y/N**
Consistently happy	
Feel okay as a person	
Believe in themselves	
Look forward to the future	
Enjoy the world around them	

Feel energetic and hopeful	
Feel they have the power to change things in their life	
Join in with others	
Feel happy with each success, no matter how small	
Look for ways to succeed	
Encourage others	
Respect others and their differences	
Accept that mistakes happen and can be learned from	

Look for questions where you answered 'no'.

The following are signs of low self-esteem. Complete the same process as above.

Feeling	**Y/N**
Feel unhappy	
Have no confidence in yourself	
Feel hopeless about the future	
See the bad things in the world around you	
Feel like a victim	
Feel miserable	
Feel tired most of the time	
Lounge about	
Put yourself down when someone gives you a compliment	
Look on the worst side of everything	
Have no respect for yourself	

Look for questions where you answered 'yes'.

If you answered any of them with a 'yes', then you have an issue that needs dealing with. Move forward to the next action and see if it works for you.

Action—Assess your own self-esteem ... and be the adult

If you are a person whose level of self-esteem is linked to your child's performance, then you need to do something about it very quickly. Don't think for a minute that your kid doesn't pick up on the cues you are giving. They know full well when thier mum and dad is happy or sad, angry or glad.

A young person's life is a rollercoaster as it is. They don't need an out-of-control parent driving the car they are sitting in.

The best place to start is by asking some serious questions that force you to be honest with yourself.

Activity 7—Self-reflection

On the table below, tick the statements that apply to you. (Note the questions don't ask 'I am happy *for* my child'. This is about *your* happiness.)

	Self-reflection	**Y/N**
1	I am happy because my child is happy	
2	I am happy because I simply love watching them play	
3	I am happy because my child played well	
4	I am happy because my child played better than another child	
5	I am happy because my child has improved	
6	I am happy because I don't like the parents from the other team	
7	I am happy because my child is the best	
8	I am happy because I feel like a better parent when they win	

9	I am happy because I was recognised as being the parent of a talented player	
10	I become more sociable when we win, or when my child does well	
11	I get sad when we don't win	
12	I am embarrassed when my child makes a mistake	
13	I would rather not talk to anyone when we lose	
14	I avoid interacting with others after a loss	
15	I go into my shell and become withdrawn when we lose	
16	I find it difficult to move on after the game	
17	My emotions fluctuate wildly during the game	
18	I get sad for the kids when they are sad	
19	I lose perspective after a loss	
20	I feel differently about my child after they lose	

This should have been a slightly difficult exercise to undertake because it forces you to look at your faults. For many people this does not come easy. Don't worry though, you don't have to show anyone the results and no-one will judge you for them.

With this in mind, go back and have another crack. Was your first answer how you truly feel, all of the time? Can you come up with a time when you *did* experience one of these responses, even slightly? It's important to acknowledge, because even though this may not be your standard reaction, the one time you did feel this way may be the time that sticks in your child's mind.

As general guide, you should not have ticked 'yes' to the following questions: 4, 6, 7, 8, 9, 10, 11, 12, 13, 14, 15, 16, 17, 19, 20.

Identified an issue?

Just like we mentioned earlier, if you merely *intend* to fix an issue, nothing will change. It will only be fixed when you actually *do* something.

If you aren't sure what to do about your issue, then have a look at the list of suggested actions below.

- Find time to be by yourself during or after the game to regain composure. A quick trip to the loo should do it.
- Repeat a phrase in your head, such as 'it's only a game' over and over again.
- Actively move on with your life. Focus on what you and your family are going to do after the game.
- Stay at home for a game or two to realise what you are missing.
- Buddy up with someone who can tell you quietly to pull your head in when you get wound up.
- Force yourself to stand with the other parents. Stop moving away and hiding.
- Commit to cheering for both teams' good plays. Commit to displaying outstanding sportsmanship for the entire time you are at the game.
- Commit to thanking the ref after the game.
- Find something to talk about other than the game with the other parents.
- Keep track of your whining—is it all you do? Balance negative comments with good ones and ensure the good ones win.
- Volunteer for a duty such as linesperson, runner, water-person, or canteen—anything that will keep your mind active and occupied.

Note that the changes you make don't have to be huge life changes. Thanking the ref after the game may simply cause you to come across as more magnanimous and sporting. It is hard to do this when you are fuming. So don't fume, be sporting.

It doesn't just have to be about your emotions, either.

Why should a trip to the ice cream shop be just for when you win? Take the kids there after a loss and you will soon see how quickly they manage to regain perspective, helping you to do the same. If all else fails, be the adult—be the parent. Suck it up and do the right thing.

I will mention this often: Kids' sports are about the kids—not you.

The key is identifying the triggers that indicate your own identity is wrapped up in your child's performance. As hard as it may be when your child makes a game-losing blunder, don't run away to hide in your car. Instead, go up and talk to the other parents. Choose how you react to the situation, and you may just help all the other mums and dads who are also stewing.

I am not saying you have to walk up and be the life of the party as if it's a great thing they lost. But keep things in perspective and let the parents know that, as bad as they are feeling, the kids are probably feeling worse. It is your job as parents to build them back up and make sure they don't lose perspective.

A good question to ask yourself is, *what reaction will best benefit my child?* If it isn't the one that you are currently exhibiting, then implement it. Simple as that.

In many ways, you have to practice what you preach. We ask our kids to be role models on the field, so why shouldn't *we* be role models off the field?

Time and time again I have seen young athletes walk over to their parents after a loss or poor game with heads down, almost in fear of the reaction they will receive. Seeing it almost makes me want to cry.

Then again, those tears of sadness turn to tears of anger when I see a parent ignore the child completely, or worse still, see them stand there until another parent points out that, 'I think your dad is sitting in his car.' No child should finish a game and then fear the reaction of their parents because, without exception, fear has no place in children's sport.

Activity 8—Being in tune with yourself

Above, we listed some simple actions you can take to help pull you out of a downward spiral. There are some deeper, more lasting strategies that you can apply to not only your sporting life but your life in general.

One such strategy involves a technique called 'mindfulness'.

Mindfulness is a state of active, open attention to the present. When you're mindful, you observe your thoughts and feelings without judging them as *good* or *bad*. Instead of letting your life pass you by, mindfulness means living in the moment and awakening to experience. Only when you have your mind 'in the moment' will you be conscious enough to note that your self-esteem has changed due to the actions of others.

Importantly, you must adopt a non-judgmental response to your own thoughts. In other words, don't suddenly start thinking you are a bad person because you were excited the other player made a mistake—just note that this is what you are thinking and gently change it to a more appropriate thought pattern. In this way thoughts become transient. You can choose to keep thinking about them or you can let them move on, replacing them with another thought.

The intended result is to destigmatise your thoughts and to stop your mind from wandering into places that put unnecessary stress on your body. You will also be able to stop yourself from having fictitious conversations in your head. You know the ones—when you imagine all the ways you are going to admonish the coach if he takes your kid off; what you are going to say if your kid doesn't get selected for the rep team; or what happens if your kid doesn't win a trophy at the end of the year. Oh, the fun you'll have giving them a piece of your mind!

All these fictitious thoughts have the power to negatively affect your demeanour and studies show they can elicit levels of stress equal to actual events.

Being mindful of your thoughts allows you to recognise when this is happening and pull yourself out of the spiral.

I haven't spoken much about my wife so far, but I don't think she will mind me mentioning this example: She has a habit of starting difficult conversations in her head before an event have even happened. For example, she will sometimes say, 'If this coach does that to our daughter, I am going to blah, blah, blah.' As she speaks, I can see her getting more and more agitated. I have to stop and remind her that yes, that would be a bad thing to do—but why are you getting riled up when he hasn't even done it yet, or is unlikely to do it at all? All that stress, angst and worry over something that hasn't even happened.

These fictitious thoughts, conversations and even arguments can invade our heads at the most inopportune times. It is a real skill to firstly recognise what's happening and then to do something about it.

If you are one of the many people who can relate to this scenario, you may want to consider some of the techniques below.

1. **Breathe**. Stop and pay attention to your breathing. When you do this, you are no longer concentrating on the game or your child … it's just you and your breath. This stops you from thinking too far ahead, giving you the chance to focus on your current emotional state and assess if it is appropriate for the situation.
2. **The NOW technique.** Follow the steps below.
    - **Notice:** Right now—what is the focus of your attention?
    - **Observe:** What are you doing right now? For example, *I am standing, I am sitting, I am walking, I am listening, I am watching sport.*
    - **Wise mind:** What state of mind should I have right now? For example, *I want to not feel angry because our kids lost.*
3. **Trigger technique**. If you find yourself getting swept up in the emotions of the game, have a 'trigger'—specifically, an object—in your pocket. Every time you feel the object, bring your thoughts back and focus on how you are feeling. Are your feelings appropriate for the situaton? Some people keep a small pebble in their pocket. Some set their phone to vibrate. Others use the sirens on the field as an opportunity to pull themselves out of the moment.

4. **Helper**. Ask someone you trust to keep an eye on you. Most coaches have a calming influence close to them during games so there's no reason why parents shouldn't have the same. When I was an Assistant Coach for St Kilda FC, one of my jobs in the coaches box was to give the Head Coach a discreet tap on the leg whenever his temper started to spike. It can be a scary assignment at times but it's an important role.

There are many good apps you can now purchase or download for free that will help you with each of the above. A common mindfulness app is called *Smiling Mind*. It has a range of short meditations that help you become more mindful. Again, being mindful shouldn't be something you switch on and off when you get to the field or court. It's something you should be practicing at all times, as it has the ability to help you at work, play, in relationships and—most importantly—in your parenting.

Now it's time to put yourself on the line and choose a technique to try. The first one you choose may not work for you. That's okay—if it's important for you to get better, then choose another one. Keep going until you find one that works. However be careful not to blame the technique for not working and not yourself for not *making* it work. Usually it is the latter that is the cause, and not the former.

The technique/s I will try this season:

1. ______________________________

2. ______________________________

Chapter 3—Summary

Do you shy away from other parents when your kid makes a mistake? Are you friendlier to them when your kid is doing well? Are the Facebook posts to let people know what they are up to, or to brag? Is the thought of missing a game as bad as having a limb amputated?

If so, you may have an issue.

There are some things you can do as a parent to ensure you give them every chance to have a strong and appropriate level of self-esteem.

- **Don't assume**. One of the biggest issues with coaches and parents is that they assume the child knows what they are thinking.
- **Treat them with respect.** Nobody likes to be disrespected, and if you want respect, then treat others with respect.
- **Avoid comparisons**. Nobody, whether you are an adult or child, likes being compared unfavourably to another person. If you have to compare, make it about a skill.
- **Relative Age Effect can be instrumental**. The REA refers to the differences in children seemingly of the same age because they play in the same team. However, a child born in January could be in a vastly different growth phase than a child born in November of the same year. Comparing these kids can be highly damaging to their psyches.
- **See problems as a chance to improve**. Many parents and coaches want to ignore personal problems when it is time for sport. A better way to look at it is to see personal problems as chance to get to know the athlete or child better.
- **Don't equate self-esteem with performance.** Don't play the 'you let me down' card or link your child's performance to their value as a person. If it is a team sport, don't individualise, because it is the team that loses—not one person.

- **It's okay to challenge.** Show your child that you believe in them and that they can get to the next level. If you have a good relationship and are honest, the child will take confidence from your confidence.
- **Role-model good behaviour**. You can't do that if you have issues with your own self-esteem.

Techniques for adults

1. **Breathe**. Stop and pay attention to your breathing. When you do this, you are no longer concentrating on the game or your child … it's just you and your breath.
2. **The NOW technique.**
   - **Notice:** Right now—what is the focus of your attention?
   - **Observe:** What are you doing right now?
   - **Wise mind:** What state of mind should I have right now?
3. **Trigger technique**. If you find yourself getting swept up in the emotions of the game, have a 'trigger'—specifically, an object—in your pocket. Every time you feel the object, bring your thoughts back and focus on how you are feeling. Are your feelings appropriate for the situation?
4. **Helper**. Ask someone you trust to keep an eye on you. Most coaches have a calming influence close to them during games so there's no reason why parents shouldn't have the same.

Chapter 4

Issue: You spend money you don't have

Do you have to make sure your kid has the very latest equipment? Do you pay excessive amounts for private coaching in the hopes that it will lead to something bigger, even though there are no guarantees?

Whilst there isn't anything wrong with buying things you can afford, it becomes a problem when you buy things you *can't* afford. Hundred-dollar boots will work just as well as $300 boots.

Ask yourself *why do you do it*? And if you can't answer easily, then you may have an issue.

As parents, we spend big on our kids for two reasons: Firstly because we don't want them to go without, and secondly because we think that we are investing in their futures.

Who knows where this sports thing will lead? Maybe a professional contract, maybe a high school scholarship, or maybe even a college scholarship in the US. If we spend big on equipment and private coaches, then the likelihood of achieving these dreams will be more of a reality than if we don't.

But that investment may be misguided, according to a new study from Utah State University's Families in Sport Lab. Researchers have found that the more parents spend on youth sports, the more likely their kids are to lose interest.

'The more money folks are investing, the higher pressure kids are perceiving,' says Travis Dorsch, an Assistant Professor at Utah State's Department of Family, Consumer and Human Development. 'More pressure means less enjoyment. As kids enjoy sports less, their motivation goes down. The indirect effect is, yes, spending more money equals less motivation.'[10]

Boy, that throws a spanner in the works, doesn't it? All this time we have been thinking that if we give the kid every opportunity we can in the sport—private coaching, best equipment, a spot on all the traveling teams—then they will love the sport forever. It seems not.

This reminds me of a young boy I played cricket with growing up. Every season he would turn up with the latest top-of-the-line bat (Gray Nicolls Twin Scoop, I recall), the latest pads, gloves, Puma shoes and bag to contain all his goodies. He was the envy of the team. Only problem was that this kid didn't really like cricket—certainly not as much as his old man did. His dad was a cricket tragic that thought buying all the latest equipment would spark enthusiasm in his son. A son who simply wasn't that good at the sport and quite frankly didn't love playing it. The good news for the rest of us was that because he didn't care about the gear, the rest of the team was allowed to use it. My family could never afford a Gray Nicolls Twin Scoop, but I remember batting with one for the entire summer of 1982, thanks to my uninterested friend and his dad with the issue.

Unfortunately, after a couple of seasons, our well-kitted out mate stopped turning up and we had to make do with club issued gear. I hate to think about how much money that family wasted.

Kids' sports are costly

Australian studies are hard to find, but in the US, parents spend $100 to $500 a month for each of their children's sports activities, according to a new survey by TD Ameritrade. Yet, one in five parents spent a whole lot more—over $1000 a month per child.[11]

Over $1000 a month per kid, are you kidding?

But throw in one or two interstate tournaments, gear, coaching, petrol, and registration fees, and it quickly adds up. There is an exercise later on you can try (if you're game) that will tell you just how much you fork out per month.

Here I digress and talk about registration fees. I cannot understand why they are rising at a rate more than quadruple the inflation rate. Soccer has to be one of the most expensive sports in Australia to play these days and is in danger of shooting its growing participation rates in the foot by pricing out many families.

If it keeps going this way then youth sport, soccer in particular, will become the domain of the upper and middle class family only. My daughter recently made the switch from soccer to AFL. The registration costs for her elite AFL program were $400 compared to over $2000 for the equivalent soccer program. I understand that the AFL is awash with money at the top and it drips downward, whereas soccer is the opposite. The big problem with soccer is that it starts with the cost bar too high and will only continue to get higher. The National Premier League (NPL) junior registration starts at $2000 and averages out at nearly $3000 per season. That is quite frankly ludicrous and profiteering at its best.

Unfortunately most of the problem is due to the rapid commercialisation of youth sports. This combined with rampant paranoia amongst parents who are being told that if they don't provide their kids with additional coaching (normally by private academies with tenuous links to professional clubs), their child will, at best, be behind the eight ball—and, at worst, will have no chance of progressing in their sport.

This 'keeping up with the Joneses'-type attitude is a driving force behind the additional spending and proliferation of private sports academies. Worst still is that the 'user-pays' system in Australia means that kids are increasingly unlikely to play two sports all year-round due to the costs.

When I was growing up in the good old days, it was football and basketball in winter, cricket and Little Aths in summer. Now, with the costs associated with youth sport, there would be no way my single-income parents could afford all those sports, especially with four kids in the family. The days of playing multiple sports has died for many families, especially when even before we factor in music, singing, dancing, Scouts, swimming, Guides and all the other extracurricular activities now on offer.

One very concerning trend that only amplifies this problem is the lack of Physical Education specialists at primary school level. Growing up, every school had a PE teacher and dedicated PE lessons each week. It was during these lessons that kids were introduced to fringe sports like volleyball or baseball without having to spend the money to join a club or buy a bat and glove, and got a chance to experiment with a new game.

These days, PE teachers are as scarce as hen's teeth in our education system. The kids don't have access to various sports or psychomotor activities like they used to. For many schools, they simply cop out and offer after-school programs run by private companies—again, on a purely user-pays basis.

In my opinion the lack of PE teachers is a huge hole in our education system. If I was choosing a school for my youngsters these days, one with a healthy PE department would be at the top of the list. Not simply for the access to sports of all sorts, but for the health benefits of learning to love activity, as well as the social benefits, along with the increased confidence.

I remember as a young teacher in training I was asked to pull a year three child out of class and teach him how to skip. Not with a rope, but just skip along like you do when you're happy. This young chap couldn't get it, but after a few sessions he was skipping along; albeit a bit methodically; with the other kids each morning. The smile on his face was gold and something I will never forget. Who does this now in schools? Does anyone, or are we too interested in teaching the kids how to navigate around a computer?

Realising the dream

The facts show that only a minuscule number of junior players go on to make the grade as a professional. Again, Australia does not readily have the stats on these things, so we have to turn to the US system as a guide.

According to a recent poll from NPR, the Robert Wood Johnson Foundation and the Harvard T.H. Chan School of Public Health, 26 percent of US parents whose high school children play sports hope their child will become a professional athlete one day. Among families with an annual income of less than $50,000, that figure is 39 percent. These stats show us that of the eight million high school athletes, less than 480,000 will play sport at college. And of that 480,000, around 3 percent will go on to have a professional career. Even here in Australia, the TAC Cup is the major supplier of talent to the AFL, yet only 5 percent of TAC players get drafted each year. That's a whopping 95 percent of kids whose dreams don't get fulfilled. And this is the number one feeder comp in the land, which means every other football competition is less than 5 percent.[12]

'It's extremely difficult to make the pros; we all know that,' says Tom Farrey, the director of the Sports and Society Program at the Aspen Institute and author of *Game On: The All-American Race to Make Champions of Our Children*. Yet, in recent years, he has started to see a shift among the parents of kids playing youth sports. 'The difference is that a lot of parents today see those odds and say, "Well, I'd better get started early with my kid".'[13]

And herein lies another problem. Instead of these odds scaring parents off, it is encouraging them to do more, and earlier. We will touch on how much earlier you should start to specialise a bit later on.

Try as I did, I could find no studies which confirmed that the earlier you start on a particular sport the more chance you have of succeeding to professional level. In fact, playing multiple sports in our formative years is now a recommended pathway rather than specialising too early. I highly recommend you don't employ a Colorado company that markets a $169 test to determine a child's 'genetic predisposition' to strength or endurance sports. And don't bother with the company who makes athletic training videos for six-month-olds.

If this relates to you, it may take a shock of some sort to awaken you from your costly slumber.

Try the activity below if you're game. If not, you can be like some parents who bury their head in the sand and say they'd rather not know. They fall back on 'we just want to do what is best for our child'.

Cutting back on extra coaching and using the money for a family holiday to Sea World will create more lasting memories for your family and most likely develop a much more appreciative and well-rounded kid than six weeks of private tuition from a guy with a level one coaching degree.

Activity 9—Budget reality

Try listing the costs of your child's sport over the last twelve months.

Item	**$**
Registration	
Coaching	
Travel games (including accommodation, car hire, flights, et cetera)	
Clothing (uniforms, costumes)	
Equipment	
Petrol (kilometres driven)	
Entry fees	
Tournament registration	
Miscellaneous	
Total	

Action 1—Excelling without spending

One of the great lessons that sport teaches kids is how to make sacrifices in order to improve. The higher you travel up the sporting ladder, the more sacrifices you will be required to make.

One of the ways to teach the value of sacrifice to kids is to ensure they do occasionally miss out on things. It may be the very latest new Nike boot that costs $300, or the new racquet that Serena Williams endorses. This 'missing out' can give them a sense of appreciation for what they have, and an understanding that talent is not a matter of equipment; it's a product of hard work.

If you were shocked at the results of the budget exercise, I suggest you sit down with your child and explain the situation. Kids won't naturally grasp the concept of affording or not affording things—they just *want* things. But you will be surprised by how quickly they can understand these issues if you take the time to explain it to them: 'We can't buy you the new boots, because with registration, the tournaments, accommodation, uniform, new racquet, et cetera, et cetera, we just can't afford those particular shoes right now.'

However, in doing this you have to be incredibly careful not to make the child feel guilty for how much money you've spent on them. This can happen, especially if you have good kids who might be inclined to worry about such matters. Never say things like, 'We are spending a lot of money on this, so you had better do well.' It is far better to tell the child that you will keep spending what you can afford as long as they enjoy playing. Because when the kid has fun, the parents all have fun, and it is a win-win for everyone. By doing this the child doesn't feel like everything is dependent on them and the parents are actually getting something out of the money also.

I heard recently of an up-and-coming young Australian tennis star who stated that she is only playing to earn enough money to set up her separated parents. This is her primary motivation. I felt sorry for her, because if money is her only determinant of success, then she will miss out on so many wonderful things a young sporting life can give her. The travel, the friends, the highs, the lows, the invites, and the wonderful people she will meet—is all of this redundant if she doesn't manage to buy her parents a new house? Will she see herself as a failure? It is nice to have goals but once the goal is set you have to enjoy the journey, because not every goal is achieved; especially one as lofty as becoming a rich and famous tennis player.

It also pays to remember that whilst sports love to promote their elite pathways and tell you that if you aren't in the right squads at the right time, your dreams of sporting stardom will not be fulfilled … this is a load of garbage. If anyone out there asks you for money in return for 'being linked to a professional team', go ahead and tell them where to go.

Unfortunately, making money on kids' sports has exploded in recent years. Every second 'academy' has links to a professional outfit or can get you a trial here or there. The fact is there are no short cuts to greatness. The war for talent is well and truly alive and no professional sport worth its salt relies on one stream of talent.

As an example, I was recently commentating an AFL game in Canberra for ABC Radio. As I stepped off the plane, I ran into the legendary St Kilda recruiter John Beverage and asked him if he wanted to share a cab to the ground. John replied that he wasn't actually going to the football and that the national U/18 basketball championships were on at the Australian Institute of Sport. Naturally, I thought that he was going along to see if he could pinch a couple of the star players, but no—his aim was to list all the players who sat on the bench. But why?—because these players were most likely *not* going to go on and play at a high level in their chosen sport. However they were obviously gifted athletes if they were good enough to reach a national U/18 level. I bet none of these kids spent exorbitant amounts of money on 'AFL skill squads' when they were little, yet here the number one talent spotter in the country was flying to Canberra to watch them.

If you are good enough … you will make it. And what boots you wore when you were twelve, the racquet you had when you were eight, or the extra skill sessions you had when you were six will have nothing to do with it. Far more important than these things will be a strong work ethic, an ability to make sacrifices, a good character, and a sense of appreciation in the people that have helped them along the way—all qualities that are completely free!

If someone does say they have links to a professional team in Australia, US or Europe, then you are quite within your rights to ask them to prove it. Is it just a marketing scheme from the club or are they actually interested in finding talent? To be honest, Manchester United have far more substantial ways of finding talent than to pay some Australian guy with a bag of balls and a set of cones to locate the next Wayne Rooney for them.

Speaking of *free*, the internet has a wealth of knowledge on virtually everything these days. You can find countless videos on skill development in virtually every sport there is along with exercise plans and tips. I don't suggest you go mad and start believing everything you read but use your common sense. There is no need to pay someone a hundred dollars an hour to run your child through some soccer skills when you can get the same drills online for nothing. All it takes is some discipline to set aside a couple of afternoons a week for the child to practice. If they don't practice, then that is another issue altogether. At worst your child will appreciate you taking an interest in them and trying to help them improve.

My own daughter looks back now and recalls fondly the times we would get up early before school to work on her speed, which—according to her coach at the time—was an issue. We didn't pay anyone to do this; we did some research, got out of bed and just did it. The time we spent working together was exponentially more valuable than any marginal speed gains we achieved.

Specialising—what age is best?

It is worth noting that additional training sessions on a single sport may actually have detrimental effects on the young athlete. According to researcher David Epstein, author of *The Sports Gene: Inside The Science of Extraordinary Athletic Performance*, the number one predictor of adult-style overuse injury in a kid is that they were highly specialised.[14]

By 'highly specialised', he means concentrating on the one sport for nine months of the year like professional athletes do. It turns out that what makes the best twenty to twenty-five-year-old athlete is not what makes the best ten to twelve-year-old athlete. Who knew?

This highly structured, all year-round approach might work for a sport like golf, where it's very static, repetitive, and less reliant on what sports analysts call 'anticipatory skills' (the ability to judge a dynamic situation in motion). For the sports that *do* require anticipatory skills—which is almost all of the ones we care about—what kids actually need is a broad exposure to different types of sports early on, and only in an unstructured manner.

Epstein's findings suggest that children don't need to specialise too early on. In fact, the best thing you can do is choose a different sport for them to play for a term at school. Fortunately, most secondary schools rotate their sports each term. Playing hockey instead of soccer may be more useful to a young athlete, as it teaches gameplay in an unstructured manner. Playing touch rugby instead of netball will help with decision-making and catching skills. And let's not forget the best thing about school sport: it's free! (Albeit dying out at primary school level through the lack of Education Department investment.)

All of this flies in the face of the '10,000 hours' practice zealots, whose doctrine requires you to start on the one sport as early as you can. They believe that if you haven't shown outstanding talent at an early age, you won't have the time to make up the skill gaps required to perform at the elite level. If you ask me, the 10,000-hour rule is a load of garbage. It doesn't account for the naturally talented players versus the unnaturally talented, or the coaching levels, motivation levels, and so many other factors. Even the notion that ten minutes of perfect practice is worth more than one hour of imperfect practice isn't factored in.

Variety is best

When I was an Assistant Coach at St Kilda FC, we interviewed kids at the AFL Draft Camp. One of the questions on our list was, 'what other sports have you played?' If it was purely AFL, it went down as a cross. If the answer involved other 'invasion' sports such as basketball, soccer, hockey et cetera, then it was a plus. The benefit the kids got from learning other tactics and techniques in these sports could often be built upon to make them better decision-makers than purely AFL-entrenched kids.

And don't discount other activities such as gymnastics or swimming. Gymnastics is fantastic for building strength, flexibility and spatial awareness. You learn to leap, twist your body and land safely—skills that are translatable to so many other sports. There's also swimming, which builds cardiovascular strength without the pounding on young growing muscles, tendons and bones.

This is another reason why every primary school should have compulsory swimming and gymnastics (PMP) programs in place. In my entire seven years at Monterey High School in Frankston, I never played one game of AFL football. I did every other sport you can imagine—baseball, basketball, cricket and (much to my family's amusement), diving. My point is that doing something other than your sport of choice may be just as useful as paying for extra lessons in your sport of choice, so don't discount what schools and local councils have on offer.

Another free resource is the kids' coach. Start to use them as a resource. After all, they're probably getting paid for their time—most leagues these days require the coaches to have a minimum coaching licence and, as such, they have access to materials and knowledge. Sit down with your coach and explain your issue. For instance, 'My kid loves training and is really keen to improve a specific part of his game, but we can't afford the private sessions the other kids are doing. Can you suggest some drills they can do either before or after training; maybe at home; that will help them?' I guarantee you that a half-decent coach will be able to help, and a great coach will go out of their way to help. And best of all, none of this will cost you an extra cent.

Now I am not saying *don't* send your child for private coaching. I have at times sent my daughters off to special skill training run by a private academy. Part of this was due to a bit of paranoia at the time that they would be left behind the more skilful kids, and partly because they wanted to do it.

My most important points are *don't do it if you can't afford it*, and *don't do it if your child doesn't love it*. And even if you can afford it, still consider the other avenues to greatness that don't cost money—not to mention the overuse injuries that may be incurred through those extra sessions.

In Chapter 2 we talked about the value of resting; having a break to mentally and physically freshen up. It can do wonders for your child and, importantly, it is also completely free.

Activity1—Free avenues to greatness

Work your way through the following questions. It may take you some research before you can answer them all, but I guarantee you will surprise yourself at how readily available good resources are. If all else fails, go to your sports governing body or to the Australian Sports Council and ask them where best to find what you are after.

List all the websites that offer individual training drills for your kid's sport.

1.____

2.____

List the sports your school offers that may provide complementary skills to your kid's sport.

1.____

2.____

List the resources available to you. For example, the coach you can seek advice from.

1.____

2.____

In this section we looked at why you don't have to necessarily spend the money. In the next, we will look at ways you can *save* money.

Action 2—Money-saving tips

Now that we know how to cut out unnecessary spending, how do we deal with the costs of *necessary* spending?

Of course there will need to be some expenditure—it's hard to hit a tennis ball without a racquet and impossible to dribble without a ball—so let's look at how can we be wise about our spending, yet still procure what we need.

How to save money

Financial experts offer these tips to help save money on kids' sports.

1. **Buy used gear**. Equipment can be a huge chunk of sports spending. Search for a local sports consignment shop where you can buy and sell gear. Or go online to find used equipment on Facebook Marketplace, or eBay. Gumtree is another rapidly-growing platform for used and even new equipment. Here's just one example I found after a quick search: Nike Tiempo football boots, purchased by seller from the UK but not the right size. Never worn in a game or training. Selling for $80. Retail price at Rebel was $220.

2. **Volunteer to coach**. If your league charges a fee, volunteer as a coach or in some other capacity. By doing so, you may be able to get your fees reduced or waived.

3. **Buy non-sports supplies in bulk**. The cost of healthy snacks, bottled water and Gatorade can add up. Pool funds with other team parents to buy these items in bulk at a wholesale discount warehouse, like Costco. Maybe get a few big cold beverage containers to fill up with plain old tap water while you're at it.

4. **Start a uniform shop**. If you're like me, you probably have kids' wardrobes full of old uniforms of all shapes and sizes. Many clubs and teams ask you to buy new uniforms each year as they enjoy the profit they earn from charging you $50 for a singlet that only costs them $25 wholesale. See if you can set up a uniform swap day or second-hand stall during the pre-season. I know when I have to get my kids new school uniforms, the 'used' section gets a workout. It seems perfectly acceptable to purchase second-hand school blazers so why not second-hand soccer shirts?

5. **Seek a sponsor**. You never know unless you ask. If your team needs gear or registration subsidies so the kids can play, why not search out local businesses who may want to sponsor a team? A couple of thousand, tax deductible dollars can go a long way in junior sport terms. Some sponsors won't like to hand over money without knowing where it is going, so attach their money directly to something like buying balls, medical equipment, et cetera.

6. **Fundraise**. Most people don't fundraise because they can't be bothered. The fact is with very little effort you can get a butcher to give you or reduce the price of some snags, get a barbeque, and set up outside your local supermarket one Saturday morning—and guess what? You've earned $1000 you can put towards your team. It doesn't have to be a grand scheme or anything over-the-top. Suddenly the cost of the tournament entry goes from $50 per player down to nothing with just a morning's work. Rotary Clubs and Lions Clubs are always looking to assist local teams and selling some snags at Bunnings is a great earner on a busy weekend. Make sure the kids are the ones involved in the selling and cooking, as they need to appreciate what goes into having them run around the field each week.

7. **Shop the sales**. The best sales generally come when the seasons are over. The end of the football season is typically the best time to buy new boots. As long as your kid doesn't go through a growth spurt in the off-season, this can save you big time. At worst, you whack them up on Gumtree and get your money back. The sales are just as huge at the end of cricket season. The gear that comes out next season may have new stickers or colours on them, but

they will by and large do exactly the same job as the previous season's models.

8. **Make 'em earn it**. Instead of forking out for new gear each season, make your child pitch in by earning some money in the off-season. There's nothing wrong with saying that you will match any money they earn and pay half towards the new racquet they covet. The lessons this teaches your child cannot be underestimated, as before you know it, they will be out looking for their first car, or house. Without a quality work ethic, these things become very difficult to attain. In the worst cases they will forever be coming to you with their hand out, so it's best to set the standards early in life. Believe me, the time goes quickly, so if you manage to install a quality work ethic in your child then you are on your way to a great parenting certificate.

9. **GoFundMe**. Recently, friends of ours had a daughter travel to the UK as part an Australian School Football squad. The cost of the trip was approximately $8000 and via a GoFundMe page they raised the full amount. You will find that there are lots of people out there willing to help a good cause. The best thing is not to ask for thousands of dollars—instead, ask for small amounts from lots of people. Easy.

10. **Pay it off**. Every year we have gone to the club or governing body and asked if we can pay the kids registration or tournament costs in instalments. Every year we have been allowed to do it because as long as they know they will get their money, (usually we set up automated deductions over twelve months) they will be okay with it. And if you have more than one kid in the sport, always ask for sibling discounts. They won't advertise these things readily, but any club who values having you as a member will take this into account. If they don't, then maybe they aren't a club that will care for your kids in the right manner. Perhaps they are more interested in making a dollar than they are in the kids ... just sayin'!

If all of the above sounds like hard work and a bit too much effort, think back to the previous topic which informed us that excessive spending may be turning your kids off sport. If that doesn't fire you up, then consider this: According to research noted by Kids Play USA Foundation, female high school athletes are 92 percent less likely to get involved with drugs, 80 percent less likely to get pregnant, and three times more likely to graduate from high school than their non-athlete peers.[15]

As a father of three young girls, who so badly wants for them to lead happy and healthy lives, it is simply impossible to ignore these statistics.

But those benefits shouldn't have to cost a fortune, which is why we should all take the time to weigh the pros and cons of every sport or activity we sign our kids up for. And when we do sign them up, how much we are sacrificing to have them play.

Kids' sports come with plenty of benefits, but they shouldn't come at the expense of saving for retirement, college, or any other long-term goal.

And it's not just about money—it's about using the precious time we spend with our children in a way that we can look back on and be proud of one day.

Activity 11—Where can you save money?

Item	Idea
Boots/shoes	
Uniform	
Sponsor options	
Fundraising	
Travel options	
Registration subsidy	
Coaching	

Again, you shouldn't frequently talk about the cost of your kid's sport in a detrimental fashion in front of them. If you do, you run the risk of making them feel guilty about playing. Instead, make the discussion about being more efficient with your money and how it is important to distribute costs around the family. I'm sure your son or daughter will get a kick out of the new car you are saving for or the holiday you will all go on or even just the new second-hand trampoline you will put in the back yard.

These are the reasons why you are making smart decisions and budgeting rather than blowing it all on $300 set of boots.

If they don't get it and want the boots over everything else, then don't cave in. They may like you for it then and there but in the long run it isn't teaching your child the right life lessons—lessons that are far more valuable than a fancy pair of boots that will become redundant midway through the season.

Chapter 4—Summary

Do you have to make sure your kid has the very latest equipment? Do you pay excessive amounts for private coaching on the hope that it will lead to something bigger, even though there are no guarantees? Whilst there isn't anything wrong with buying what you can afford, it becomes a problem when you buy things you can't afford.

'The more money folks are investing, the higher pressure kids are perceiving,' says Travis Dorsch, an Assistant Professor in Utah State's Department of Family, Consumer and Human Development. 'More pressure means less enjoyment. As kids enjoy sports less, their motivation goes down. The indirect effect is, yes, spending more money and less motivation.'[16]

Unfortunately most of the problem is due to the rapid commercialisation of youth sports. This combined with rampant paranoia amongst parents who are being told that if they don't provide their kids with additional coaching (normally by private academies with tenuous links to professional clubs), their child will, at best, be behind the eight ball—and, at worst, will have no chance of progressing in their sport.

Yet, in recent years, there has been a shift among the parents of kids playing youth sports. Instead of the unfavourable odds scaring parents off, it is encouraging them to do more, and earlier. Playing multiple sports in our formative years is now a recommended, healthier pathway than specialising too early.

One of the great lessons sports teaches kids is that you have to make sacrifices in order to improve. In fact, the higher you travel up the sporting ladder the more sacrifices you have to make. One of the ways to teach the value of sacrifice is to ensure the kids do occasionally miss out on some things.

Never say things like, 'We are spending a lot of money on this, so you had better do well.' It is far better to tell the child that you will keep spending what you can afford as long as they enjoy playing.

It also pays to remember that whilst sports love to promote their elite pathways and tell you that if you aren't in the right squads at the right time, your dreams of sporting stardom will not be fulfilled … this is a load of garbage.

If you are good enough, you will make it. And the boots you wore when you were twelve, the racquet you had when you were eight, or the extra skill sessions you had when you were six will have nothing to do with it. Far more important than these things will be a strong work ethic, an ability to make sacrifices, a good character, and a sense of appreciation.

Moreover, additional training sessions on just one sport may have detrimental effects on the young athlete. According to researcher David Epstein, the number one predictor of adult-style overuse injury in a kid is that they were highly specialised.

In terms of free resources, the internet has a wealth of knowledge on virtually everything these days. You can find countless videos on skill development in virtually every sport there is along with exercise plans and tips.

Now I am not saying don't send your child for private coaching, but certainly don't do it if you can't afford it. And even if you can, think twice about it, as there are other avenues to greatness that don't cost money.

How to save money

1. Buy used gear. Equipment can be a huge chunk of sports spending.
2. Volunteer to coach. If your league charges a fee, volunteer as a coach or in some other capacity.

3. Buy non-sports supplies in bulk. The costs of healthy snacks, bottled water, and Gatorade can add up.
4. Start a uniform shop. If you're like me, you have kids' wardrobes full of old uniforms of all shapes and sizes.
5. Seek a sponsor. You never know unless you ask. Why not seek out local businesses who may want to sponsor your team?
6. Fundraise. Most people don't fund raise because they can be bothered.
7. Look for sales. The best sales generally come when the seasons are over.

If all of the above sounds like hard work and a bit too much effort, think back to the previous topic which outlined that excessive spending may be turning your kids off sport.

Kids' sports come with plenty of benefits, but they shouldn't come at the expense of saving for retirement, college, or any other long-term goal.

And it's not just about money—it's about using the precious time we spend with our children in a way that we can look back on and be proud of one day.

Keeping perspective is vital. Ensuring your child enjoys their childhood, has great memories of family time and understands their responsibility to be a good citizen is more important than any sports pathway you want them on.

Chapter 5

Issue: I know what is best

Whether it's the goals they want to achieve in an individual game or their bigger career goals, do you completely disregard what your kid wants and tell them what *you* think is best for them?

Think about your kid's goals—are they yours or theirs? If they're yours, you may have an issue.

This is an area that often causes conflict between parents and kids and in many cases can lead to lifelong divides. One of the key reasons this divide occurs is because parents tend to think about the 'bigger picture'. They see the peripheral aspects of sporting stardom, such as the pay cheques, notoriety, lifestyle, and opportunities, and can project these things for years and even decades ahead. Whereas kids tend to see what is right in front of them: a sport they have fun playing. Sure they may say, 'One day I will be a tennis star and win Wimbledon', but in terms of what drives their commitment to the sport, having fun and improving will be front of mind—far more often than potential future stardom.

Take a junior AFL player as an example. To a junior footballer the big picture is to think about how exciting it would be to represent their favourite team on the MCG one day. To the parent, the big picture is number one draft pick, five-year contracts, retirement and a cushy job in the media.

As kids get older, they are able to project their thoughts further into the future. It's not until they get to around sixteen and seventeen years old; when they also have to start thinking about jobs, college, university, and ATAR scores; that they begin to line their goals up with adults. But even then, it is not uncommon for there to be a complete disconnect between what the kid wants and what the adult wants.

It is this scenario that can drive a wedge between kids and parents. The parents can't understand why their kid doesn't want something as badly as they do, and inevitably conflict arises when the kid doesn't work at it as hard as their parents want them to work. You often hear these parents on the sidelines:

'My Josh doesn't want it badly enough—he is lazy and won't do the extra practice. I have scoped out a morning training plan for him but all he does is whinge. James over there does an extra fitness session three times a week. I have to force Josh to do *one* extra session. He won't get in the rep team, I just know it because he is a lazy bugger.'

You may think this conversation is fictional, but it is one I actually overheard. Poor little Josh, the twelve-year-old kid who probably just wants to play for fun, or actually doesn't like soccer as much as his parents want him to. Imagine the angst every morning as his mum or dad openly demonstrate their disappointment in him for not following their plan to the letter.

Knowing how damaging goal-setting can be if done incorrectly, we need to ensure we approach it in a coordinated and structured fashion—even if only to make sure that the whole exercise does not become a waste of time. Or, worse, a source of angst between you and your child.

The key to any goal-setting; the thing that will determine whether it is successful or unsuccessful; is *motivation*. You can scope out the most precise goal using whatever the modern method is—in my day it was SMART goals ('specific', 'measurable', 'action-oriented', 'realistic' and 'timely'). You can check all of these boxes with precise actions and know exactly when you are going to achieve them, but there is a major component missing: motivation.

And this is where the conflict between parent and child arises. Studies like one I mentioned from the Journal of Physical Activity and Health will show that the two most popular reasons why the children play sports are for fun, and to be with their friends.[17]

If these are their prime motivators, they are unlikely to sign up to goals that are aimed at achieving something else. They won't get it when you talk about the trappings of professional sport when all they want to do is have a good time. They will listen and nod, but they won't really understand and, most importantly, they won't work hard to meet their goals. This renders the whole goal-setting process useless.

Most of the time kids will set goals that involve improving their skills because these are easy to measure—one day they can't do it, and then the next they can.

You may think they choose skill development so they can become elite players, but more often it is just so they can become better at their sport and enjoy playing even more. Think about your mindset when you see your kid in the back yard practicing her soccer skills. In your mind, you are probably thinking *about time ... in order to reach the top she will need to improve her skills.* Whereas the child may simply be thinking, *this is fun, I'm getting so much better at juggling.*

Now let's take another look at motivation. I will use the example that many people can relate too: joining a gym. The thought of going to a gym and finally getting healthier afflicts us all at some stage. We go along to our nearest gym, sign up, pay our membership, and go four times in the first week. The following week we also go four times, but in the third week we drop down to three times. After that, our attendances drops to twice a week, then once a week, and six weeks later we're at the front desk trying to get our money back. Sound familiar? The reason why this happens is the goal of 'getting fit' does not have sufficient motivation behind it, and you lose sight of your determination.

The same thing will occur if you set your child's goals for them. Because they won't have the same motivations as you, they will drop off almost straight away. Just like you at the gym.

The worst possible outcome in this situation is that you turn into the nagging parent who berates your child for not practicing more or doing whatever is required to meet their goals (*your* goals). They turn to you with a *really, Dad?* expression and either ignore you, or train under protest. The only one who feels good about the situation is you, because you now feel like your child has taken a step closer to realising their potential. In fact, they have more than likely taken a step *away* from reaching their potential by losing a bit of passion for their chosen sport.

Being the nagging parent is a sure-fire way to drive a wedge between you and your child. In the most extreme cases, you will lose any form of relationship you have with them, forever. Just think about how you would feel if you had a person nagging you to go to the gym; calling you fatty and saying that you will probably never have a good life because you quit the gym. You wouldn't appreciate or tolerate that for very long, would you?

Whatever happened to ...?

There are many examples throughout history of players who no longer have anything to do with their nagging, pushy parents. Some of them did end up making it big, others had fleeting careers, but many more burnt out before they ever got there. These are the ones you have never heard of but get spoken of when people say, 'Whatever happened to ...?'

One sad story comes from Australian swimming legend Leisel Jones.

Jones has admitted she felt 'no sadness' after finding out her father had passed away as they were 'never close'.

The swimmer, who successfully claimed nine Olympic medals across four separate Games, opened up about her private battle with depression in 2004. She released a memoir called *Body Lengths*, detailing the overwhelming pressure and constant taunting she endured during her career.[18]

She revealed that she was 'actively encouraged to skip meals' in an effort to lose weight as a teen and felt often ridiculed in front of her peers at thrice weekly weigh-ins, where coaches used code words to call the young athletes 'fat'.

She writes, 'Whenever I have to stand on the pool deck in my togs, listening to my body being discussed like it's an engine and not the arms, legs, thighs and stomach of a teenage girl, I am self-conscious and miserable.'

Jones said girls would often sob in the showers after they were 'weighed, weighed and weighed again' as men 'as old as our dads' would pass judgement.

This is just one of a litany of sad sports stories involving young athletes and their parents. The world of tennis has more than its fair share of parent disaster stories. Nearly every tennis pro will tell you stories about kids they grew up playing against who had nightmare parents, some of whom are no longer involved in the game. Personally I can't think of anything worse than not having a healthy relationship with my children, and no amount of sporting success could make up for not having them in my life.

The other thing to remember is that kids can't think long term. Why would we want them to? Isn't it better for them to enjoy being kids right now, before the worries and concerns of adulthood descend upon them? Of course it is, so why do we insist on making them think about the future?

When my eldest daughter finished high school, we'd have loved a dollar for every time somebody asked either of us, 'So what are you going to do now?' You should've seen some of the strange looks we got when her answer was, 'I am not sure yet.' I told them she had plenty of time and just needed to find that one thing she enjoyed doing and was most passionate about. Still, many people couldn't believe that at age seventeen, she didn't have her entire future mapped out for her.

Not all advice is good advice

I was giving a talk at a girls' high school not long ago when the speaker before me, a winter Olympian, preached to the girls that they had to develop a ten-year plan in order to be successful. Yes, a ten-year plan … and these were thirteen-year-old girls!

Goodness me—it took all of my strength to get up after her and tell the girls to please ignore everything they had just heard. Instead, be kids, enjoy yourselves, be good to your parents and enjoy what you do. If you don't enjoy it then stop it and find something else to do. End of speech. Mic drop.

Activity 12—Your kid's goals

Write down what you think your kid's goals should be.

This season.

1.____

2.____

3.____

Next five years.

1.____

2.____

3.____

Now put yourself into the mind of your kid. What do you honestly think *they* would write down as their goals if they knew they wouldn't have to show them to you or the coach? What would they really want to get out of playing?

This season.

1.____

2.____

3.____

Next five years.

1.____

2.____

3.____

If you have no idea what they would say, then you have some work to do. Is it because you haven't listened to them about why they play? Is it because you have been too busy determining their goals for them? Is it because you just don't know your kid well enough?

Whatever the reason, I suggest you start to pay more attention to what your kid is saying, what makes them happy and—importantly—decide if you need to step back. They *should* come to you if they need help.

Action 1—How to set goals with kids

If you must go down the goal-setting path, it is vital to understand that your kid's goals must be your kid's goals. Whilst you think you know what is best for them, you probably don't know what motivates them, and without significant motivation the goal will be useless.

You will end up like Earl Woods, the father of Tiger Woods. Earl would demand that Tiger hit a certain amount of practice shots after school before he was allowed to come to the dinner table. This was just one of the numerous demands and expectations he placed on a very young child. A child that from the age of four was on national television programs, being hailed as the next big thing in world golf. I ask you, can a four-year-old child decide to be the world's next greatest golfer?

My question is, did this make Tiger the champion golfer he was, or did it contribute to his sense of entitlement and disastrous personal life? You may say it helped him become the world's best golfer, but do you really think Earl and Tiger were the only parents and kids out whacking balls for hours a day? Not a chance, and yet, where are all those other kids now? (Hopefully, still talking to their dads.)

The same can be said for the Williams sisters, Venus and Serena. We have seen and heard stories about their father insisting the girls focus on tennis from a ridiculously early age. Do you think he was the only parent in America or around the world doing that? Again—no, he wasn't. Would the kids have been as good as they are now without the push? Who knows, but what I *do* know is that there are far more kids who missed out on a normal childhood because of an overbearing sports parent than there are Woods and Williams.

So if you think that this is the only way to get ahead in your sport—by copying the Woods and Williams families—then please reconsider.

I have a rule in my house that I am willing to go outside and have a kick of the footy wherever and whenever you want. *I*, however, won't be waking you up to do it. You must wake *me* up, because if you don't, I will stay in bed. This way the kids are in control of their training and not succumbing to a pushy sports dad.

This doesn't mean you shouldn't help your child set goals. It basically depends on what sort of goals they are setting.

If their coach says to set a goal for the game, or for the first half of the season, they may need some help. Many will just write down what they think the coach wants to hear, such as 'improve my first touch' in soccer, or 'improve my backhand' in tennis. You can steer them away from the generic responses and in the right direction by asking some simple questions such as:

Question to ask	Reason for asking
What do you really like about playing?	Narrow down what exactly they find fun about the game. This way, the goal can correspond with these 'fun' actions.
Which parts do you not like about playing?	They may not like something because they simply don't do it very well. A little bit of focused practice could be all that is required to turn this arounds.
What parts are you really good at?	Goal-setting doesn't always have to be about improving deficiencies. It can include making strengths even stronger.
What do you think you need to improve on?	Self-appraisal is an important skill. Their answer may not be the number one thing you think they need help with, but your opinion doesn't count.

The key is to only use the above technique if and when the child obviously needs help. A good coach will help them correct their weaknesses whether they have it written down on a piece of paper or not. I get terribly frustrated with coaches who see weaknesses in a child's techniques and uses that as a reason why they don't get promoted or given additional support.

If a coach ever says to you, 'We can't put your child in the team because her backhand is not up to scratch', you are well within your rights to say, 'Okay, what are you, the coach—the person I am paying, the person hired by the club—doing to correct this deficiency?' Never let them pigeonhole your child until they have done everything within their power to assist them.

Avoid labels

On this point, avoid having anyone (yourself included) put labels on your kids. Labels such as 'slow', 'can't kick', and 'only a defender' can become self-fulfilling and destroy a kid's confidence. Just like if you call a kid 'funny'—pretty soon, they will drive you mad trying to live up to the 'funny kid' label. Same as calling kid 'shy'—doing so gives the kid licence to be shy and will therefore remain so. If you want your kids to be confident, then think about the labels you have assigned to them and how these labels may be holding them back.

In the end you may not agree with the goals they have set. But you know what? It doens't really matter.

The vital *why*

The question of '*why* did you write that particular goal?' is very rarely asked. However, I believe it is a crucial question to successful goal-setting for kids. What you are trying to do is get to the motivation behind the goal. Remember previously we spoke about the importance of motivation. Asking *why* they want to achieve something will help both you and your kid reinforce their goal for when they can't be bothered.

Here's an example:

Little Josh has written a goal that he wants to be able to dribble the basketball with his non-dominant hand. He puts together a plan to be able to do this by practicing for twenty minutes, three times a week.

After school, he comes home, switches on his PlayStation and forgets about his dribbling time. As a parent, we scold him for not following through and risk making him resent the fact that he set the goal in the first place. This is a common scenario—one that elicits comments like, 'He obviously doesn't want it badly enough'. Or, worse still, 'He is a lazy bugger'.

However, if you had asked Josh *why* he wants to learn to dribble with his non-dominant hand, he may have answered with, 'It's so I can play point guard, as they get to bring the ball down the court, which is pretty fun. At the moment we have to let Ben do it as he is the only one who can dribble with both hands.'

Knowing this, you can remind Josh of the fun he could have playing point guard, and then let him make up his own mind as to whether this motivation is strong enough to turn off the PlayStation. You haven't nagged, but rather reminded him of what *he* will get out of a bit of extra practice. Without knowing his 'why', you run the risk of becoming that nagging parent nobody wants to be or to have.

Keep it simple

I often laugh when I hear about junior coaches getting the children to write down five goals they want to work on over the season, and then list the multitude of things they are going to do to achieve these goals. Quite frankly they have made a complete balls-up of the whole process, as no kid can follow that system—no matter how studious they are.

Think of yourself at work when the boss makes you sit through a goal-setting session. How long do these goals stay at the forefront of your mind? And you are probably getting *paid* to attain them. I bet the next time you look at them will be right before your performance evaluation time, at which point you'll scramble to knock a couple off and find excuses as to why you haven't done the rest.

Kids are the same, so if you are a coach or parent who is asking your kids to set goals, don't set and forget. And whatever you do, don't overcomplicate the process.

As a general guide, kids' goals should be organised by age appropriate goal-setting.

Age	Goals	Reason
10 years and under	Have fun	That is all they should be concerned with
11–12 years	Have fun + 1 short-term goal	Short-term is something they can achieve within a **fornight** For example, get ten juggles of the succer ball, hit four serves in a row over the net, dribble the ball left-handed up and down the court
13–15 years	Have fun + 1 short-term goal + 1 medium-term goal	Short term—need to see quick results as kids can't focus on slow improvements without risk of losing patience and desire Similar goals to above, but fifty juggles instead of ten, and so on Medium term goal—**two months**. Even this may be a stretch and should only be used for elite-level kids. Anything longer than two months will seem like a lifetime away
16–18 years	Have fun + 2 short-term goals + 1 medium-term goal + 1 long-term goal	As above, but kids this age can also start thinking longer-term. Long term—goals they can attain by the **end of the season.**

Note that we haven't asked the kids to put down any goals longer than the season duration. This is purely because one of the key parts of goal-setting is measurement. A goal, if it is going to be worthwhile, involves measuring your progress and outcome. A long-term goal like two, three, four, or five years down the track is too far away to actively measure. And if you don't measure it and evaluate your progress, then the child *and* the adults will forget about it.

Aspirations

A far better way to look at things is to *aspire* to an achievement, such as making a representative team, get drafted, play for your state, make the first team, et cetera. Your goals should be stepping-stones to achieving what you aspire to achieve.

For example, your year nine child may aspire to make the school's first-grade netball team by the time she leaves school. The first team is something she aspires too. The goals she meets along the way will ensure she gets there.

Ask her to set short-term goals, or steps she will take in order to get there.

These could include goals such as:

1. Improve my passing strength.
2. Improve my agility.
3. Keep loving my netball.

Now, just add in the actions you are going to take to make this happen. For example:

1. Twenty push-ups every night for thirty days to build up arm strength. (Keep going until I can do twenty without stopping.)
2. Twenty squat lunges each night for thirty days to build up leg strength.
3. Attend training with my friends every session.

When you think about it, it is the stuff she will do in each thirty-day block that will get her in the first team for netball—*not* simply writing down 'I want to be in the first team'.

Using the word 'aspire' rather than 'goals' has a better ring to it for me, so try using it with your kids. I want my kids to aspire to things and then set goals to reach them.

Performance and outcomes

Olympic athletes will tell you that they concentrate on the outcome for about 20 percent of the time at most. Eighty percent of their focus is on *performance*—what they actually have to do to achieve the outcome. The ones who are considered elite are the ones who perform at a consistently high level and in all conditions. You can only be consistent and in all conditions when your focus is on performing—not the outcome.

I was reminded of the power of focusing on performance rather than outcomes when watching a rowing regatta on television a little while ago. A single scull rower who was heavily favoured to win the race found herself two lengths behind at the halfway mark. Slowly and surely, she made her way through the field and by the finish line was a slim 1 metre ahead. She had virtually come out of nowhere.

After the race the commentator asked her about her thoughts at the halfway mark. Specifically, did she think she could catch the boat in front? Her response was something along the lines of this: 'I couldn't control what was happening in the boat in front. All I could control was making sure my oar hit the water at exactly the right angle on every stroke. That's all I could control—my performance. If that was good enough to catch them then it was. So that's all I thought about.'

It was a perfect example of focusing on what you have to *do* to get the outcome and not the outcome itself. Doing the latter; focusing on the outcome; is the reason why so many athletes and teams choke in big games. They forget about what they need to do in order to win and instead focus on the end result. In other words, they try to make up the difference by rowing harder because they are losing and subsequently their oar hits the water at any old angle as they panic about not achieving the result they wanted.

Action 2—Five goal-setting tips from left field

Here are some left field points to remember about goal-setting for kids:

1. Realistic. Cutting ten seconds of your best time or driving a golf ball and extra 50 metres may sound like great things to achieve, but when you expect to do it in a month, you may be setting yourself up to fail. Many coaches and parents would say that's ridiculous—you could never achieve that. But you know what? Who cares! The most important part of the conversation is not what they are going to achieve but *how* they are going to achieve it—the action. Work out and plan the 'how', follow it through, and I guarantee that there will be improvement when the time is up.

The conversation is not then 'I told you so' or 'you didn't get your goal', but, 'Well done on your hard work—have a look where you were one month ago and now look at how much you have improved. Great stuff!' Regarding the missed goal, all you need to say is, 'Maybe the time frame to achieve that goal was a bit short, you can still cut ten seconds off or drive the ball 50 metres further. It will just take more practice, so let's plan again.'

And remember what Confucius apparently once said: 'When it is obvious that the goals cannot be reached, don't adjust the goals, adjust the action steps.'

2. Growth mindset. A 'growth mindset' thrives on challenge and sees failure not as evidence of unintelligence, but as a heartening springboard for growth and for expanding our existing abilities. Carol Dweck, who pioneered growth mindset studies, writes, 'Why waste time proving over and over how great you are, when you could be getting better? Why hide deficiencies instead of overcoming them? Why look for friends or partners who will just shore up your self-esteem instead of ones who will also challenge you to grow? And why seek out the tried and true, instead of experiences that will stretch you? The passion for stretching yourself and sticking to it, even (or especially) when it's not going well, is the hallmark of the growth mindset. This is the mindset that allows people to thrive during some of the most challenging times in their lives.'[19]

I used this method when I was coaching junior Life Savers one summer. I would challenge them constantly by asking things like, 'Who can swim around the far cans?' Initially they all replied, 'I can't swim that far.' To promote a growth mindset, the new answer they had to give was, 'I can't swim that far ... yet.' Adding the 'yet' made all the difference. We would then plan a course over the coming weeks to ensure that the kids could do it, and when they were ready, we would let them try. You should've seen their faces when they did it—especially compared to the fright when I first asked them if they could. In short, a person with a growth mindset will not say 'I can't'. They will say, 'I can't ... yet!'

3. Base them on action, not outcome. Avoid goals like, 'I won't get angry on the pitch or crack it with an umpire.' These are the *outcomes* of certain actions. If you want to have better behaviour on the pitch, make a goal that involves a specific action—for instance, 'I will acknowledge the umpire's good decisions.' This is far more proactive than simply saying, 'I won't yell at the umpires.' Otherwise it becomes like the old *don't think of an elephant* trick. Sure enough, the first thing you think about when someone says that is an elephant. Best to say, 'I will acknowledge all good decisions' rather than simply telling yourself, 'Don't yell at the umpire.'

4. Visibility. I reckon about 99.9 percent of all goals kids set are forgotten about within a week—mainly because they are put out of sight and therefore out of mind. Even as adults we do this. Make sure the short-term goals are kept somewhere visible like the fridge, bathroom mirror, or on the bedside table. Additionally, the best goals will allow the child to go back and fill in progress along the way. If the goal is to juggle a soccer ball fifty times, allow them to write down every increase in personal best on the journey to that fifty. Stick the improvements on the fridge and encourage them for every step closer to fifty they get. Every time they get one more it's a cause for celebration. Kids like to show you how they have improved—the fridge is a great place for just that.

When Australian swimming ace Mack Horton was growing up, he had all of Kieran Perkins' and Daniel Kowalski's junior 1500-metre records written on a piece of paper he stuck to his bedroom roof. This way he could lie there after training and remind himself of why he was working so hard. As he passed each one, he would tick them off and then plan his performance to beat the next one.

5. Rewards. It is your job as parent to notice when your kids do well and reinforce the behaviour. How else do they learn to be good citizens? When your child takes a step toward attaining their goal, give them some love with a 'well done' or piece of encouragement. Don't go overboard and fork out for a new racquet because your kid won a set in tennis—keep things in perspective—but remember, even as adults we appreciate a 'well done' from a person we respect more than a grand, infrequent gesture. For our example of trying to juggle the ball fifty times, never say, 'I see you still haven't gotten fifty yet.' Say, 'You are getting closer to fifty, keep up the great work and you'll get there.' The reward for such an effort may be as simple as a genuine show of excitement when they achieve a goal.

I say *genuine* because the kids can tell when you are faking it. It doesn't have to be a brand new $200 pair of boots and the whole world doesn't need to know about it. Showing that *you* are proud of the effort they put into achieving the goal is vital, so don't make it all about the fifty. The numerous nights of practice are what is important—that commitment is the key lesson they need to take away from the process. Be genuine and whatever you do, don't buy the $200 boots because they got forty juggles. Think of the lesson this sends: *Near enough is good enough.*

I asked my daughters, who had a juggle record list stuck on our fridge, what the best thing was about putting up a new record. They said it was the initial excitement about their improvement and then sharing it with the rest of us who would be genuinely happy for them. In this case there was no need to bribe them with expensive gifts in order to get them to practice.

Finally, if you must set goals, always make sure the first one is to *enjoy your sport*. If you enjoy your sport then you will go to training and you will practice by yourself at home—*that* is what will make you better. Not filling in a goal sheet because the coach said you had to.

Activity 13—Goal-setting template

Use this template when helping your child set goals. For the number of goals, see age-appropriateness table on previous pages.

Specific goal	Why?	How?	When?	Reward
Make it measurable. For example, reduction in tome, increased skill, et cetera	This is your motivation	Max: three points. Try to do more than three and you will get none of them done!	See table on age appro-priateness	Everyone loves a reward. Make the reward within your control—not something like 'I will get picked for the A-team'. That may be out of your hands

As stated, the reward should be something within your control. My own daughter had a goal to make the School Sport Victoria State Soccer team. After an injury interrupted her pre-season, she was behind the eight ball and worked her backside off to get back in the team. For her, the reward was a spot in the team, but unfortunately—despite all the hard work—she missed out. Did she deserve the spot? Possibly yes. But whether or not she got in was, at the end of the day, out of her hands. The only thing she could control was whether she was doing everything possible to get back into the team. This is what she should have been rewarded on—not something out of her control like the selection thoughts of a coach she doesn't know.

We as parents managed to make her see what valuable lessons she learnt along the way about resilience and fighting for what you want. In the end these lessons were far more valuable than getting picked for a game that, in years to come, she probably won't remember playing in.

It is vitally important that kids don't feel like failures if they don't achieve a goal. This is also why I like the idea of 'aspiring to' something, as it is less time-bound. The good news was my daughter made the team the following year—aspiration attained.

For the older kids who are setting longer-term goals, you can add in a 'milestone' section. Times where you will stop and reflect and possibly adjust your plan. Remember what Einstein said about the definition of stupidity—it's doing the same thing over and over again and expecting a different result.

Older kids especially need to assess their plan. You can only do this if you make the steps measurable, which allows you to keep track of your improvements.

Action 3—Don't fuel their doubts

'Your skills are improving, so in this game make sure you do a "step over" to get around your opponent.'

This is a phrase many of us have said to our soccer kids over the years. I know I have said it to all three of my girls. Although my intention was to give them a pump up, I may have been fuelling their doubts.

An instruction such as 'make sure you do a step over', may be designed to help them play well, but there is a chance all the kid hears is, *Oh no, now playing well means I have to do tricky stuff, too.*

As the weight of expectation goes up, the confidence levels can come down—especially when the expectation involves mastering actions that could make them look silly if they fail. Sports psychologists tell us that athletes who expect too much of themselves often have trouble dealing with 'minor errors'. This is a problem, as minor errors are a natural part of every sport.

The scenario in these players' minds looks like this:

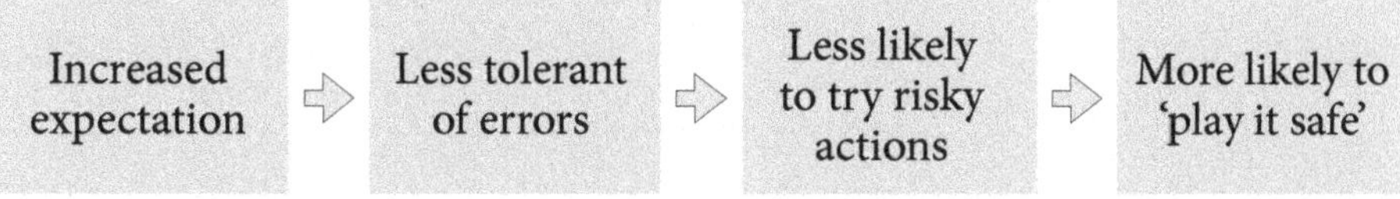

A better approach is to play the 'long game'.

- Give them plenty of opportunity to practice and take note of when they improve.
- During the week, plant the seed that they should try this skill in the game, but never tell them to do something new right before they take the field.

- Give them permission to stuff it up. Expect the three-pointer to be an air ball, or the step over to go completely awry.
- Reward the attempt, not the outcome.
- Laugh off the stuff-ups.
- Do whatever you can to take the pressure off the perfect performance of the skill, such as working with the coach so that they are teaching the same message as you—that it is okay to fail and that persistence at training is the answer. Eventually (it could take many weeks) the ball will go in the hoop or the step over will bamboozle an opponent. This will give them more confidence than any words of encouragement you can offer.

This is what I mean by playing the long game. It will happen, just in their time frame—not yours. Expecting a player to make significant, immediate changes to their game doesn't work with most kids. Of course some kids are more willing to try and fail than others. The key is knowing what works best for your child, not for you as their parent.

Note: the long game does not apply to non-negotiable expectations such as effort, sportsmanship, listening to coaches, and following team rules.

Chapter 5—Summary

Think about your kid's goals and see if they are yours or theirs. If they're yours, then you have an issue.

The key to any goal-setting is motivation.

Kids are unlikely to sign up to goals that don't correspond with their personal motivations. They won't get it when you talk about the trappings of professional sport when all they want to do is have fun.

The worst possible outcome in this situation is that you become a nagging parent who berates your child for not practicing more or doing whatever is required to meet their goals. Being the nagging parent is a sure-fire way to drive a wedge between you and your child and, in the most extreme cases, irreparably damage your relationship.

The other thing to remember is that kids can't think long term. Why would we want them to? Isn't it better for them to enjoy being kids right now, before the worries and concerns of adulthood descend upon them?

Understand that your kid's goals have to be your kid's goals. Whilst you think you know what is best for them, you don't know what motivates them. And without significant motivation their goal will be useless.

The question of *why* your kid chose a particular goal is very rarely asked. However I believe it is crucial factor in successful goal-setting for kids, as it helps determine their primary motivation. Asking why they want to achieve something will help the both of you in keeping their goals on track.

For kids, their goals should be viewed as stepping-stones to achieving what they aspire to achieve.

Here are some left field points to remember about goal-setting for kids:

1. **Realistic.** The most important part of the goal-setting conversation is not what they are going to achieve but how they are going to do it.
2. **Growth mindset.** A growth mindset thrives on challenge and sees failure not as evidence of unintelligence but as a heartening springboard for growth and for stretching our existing abilities.
3. **Visibility.** 99.9 percent of all goals that kids set are forgotten about within a week, mainly because they are put out of sight and therefore out of mind.
4. **Rewards.** It is your job as parent to notice when your kids do well and reinforce the behaviour.

Play the long game when it comes to improvement. Being in a hurry for kids to improve may be doing them a disservice as many kids improve at different rates. Avoid comparing them with other kids who may be in different stages of development. Remember the junior champion who stopped growing and his career halted? We all know one.

Finally, if you must set goals, always make sure the first one is to *enjoy your sport.*

Chapter 6

Issue: Fear Of My Child Missing Out (FOMCMO)

Do you want your kid to be the big fish in the little pond, or is it always somebody else's fault why your kid is not over-achieving?

If so, then you may have an issue.

We all know the kid who has moved from team to team every year. It is impossible to keep track of where they are from season to season. They become topics of discussion when parent groups get together, where the phrase 'I don't blame the kid, I blame the parents' is bandied around.

If you do get a chance to speak to the parents, they will tell you the change was made for one of the following reasons:

- They didn't get along with the coach.
- Their child's talents weren't identified.
- Their child wasn't 'being developed'.

Quite often the real reason is simply because the child was not given a free ride by the coach or made the centre of attention. Instead of persisting and fighting through, they choose to run to greener pastures. In 90 percent of cases, it isn't the child who makes the decision to leave. It's the parent.

If you fall into this category, start by asking yourself, *who suggested the move*—you, or your kid?

Furthermore, what were the motives behind your move? Were you like the father in the suburbs of Philadelphia who sued his son's high school track coach for forty million dollars after the teen was cut? The man claimed his son's chances of getting a college scholarship were badly damaged.[20]

Or are you like the Dallas-area father who filed a racketeering lawsuit against an elite lacrosse camp, accusing officials of intimidating players into attending? He cited as evidence the fact that his son wasn't made an official member of the varsity team by a coach who also worked at the camp.[21]

Then there was the case of the young volleyball player who took her league to court because, after being benched by the coach, she wanted to move teams. It just so happened that the league had a rule saying you can't move teams mid-season, so she was stuck. The judge ruled that he couldn't interfere with local league rules, so she had to suck it up and learn to be a good teammate, and get better so she could get off the bench.[22]

I can see the logic driving these children's parents: If my child isn't recognised at this age, their chances of selection at higher levels will be greatly reduced. So, they *have* to play.

All examples above emanate from what I call FOMCMO—Fear of My Child Missing Out. As stated earlier, we all want what is best for our kids. What FOMCMO parents fail to see are the lessons learnt by *not* getting what you want. Often, these lessons can be more powerful and longer lasting than continually getting what you want.

The fact is selection at higher levels involves far more than whether you have the skills to play. There is a lot of talent around these days, so a coach will also be looking for good talent *and* good people, good teammates, good role models, et cetera. If it came down to a choice between a litigious person who runs to court when they don't get their own way or a selfless team person, then I reckon I know which one will get the nod.

As an example a friend of mine's daughter was recently elevated to a national level representative team. Previously she was in a shadow squad but when two players pulled out, they had to find replacements. The coach researched the next four players ranked in line (based on talent and positions) and found all of them wanting in the 'character' traits he was looking for. Basically he did not want to be concerned with taking eighteen-year-old girls to the UK for three weeks if they were going to cause problems. He wanted kids of good character and therefore went all the way down to the fifth player on the list, as she was the one who would fit in with the team and, importantly, not be a headache to take away.

This is a common story as I know full well the lengths AFL clubs go to in order to choose players of good character. Having worked at several prestigious secondary colleges and being involved in their sports teams, I have been a point of call from recruiters wanting to know about the kids. Not once did they ask me whether the kids could play or not or about their strengths and weaknesses. Rather, the focus was on what sort of kid they are—are the coachable, show good manners, fit in with the team, have leadership abilities?

Recruiters already know whether they can play or not as they see them running around the field every week. They are looking for a point of difference and that point is almost always *character*. Kids who swap teams from year to year often don't have the best reputations. Rightly or wrongly, it's a fact.

Do you need to change?

The downfall for kids in changing teams each year are numerous. Funnily enough, the downside for parents is not nearly as bad. Perhaps this is why they make the decisions more often than not.

For the kids, changing teams incurs:

- Difficulty in making long-term friendships.
- Less resilience and coping strategies.
- No continuity in coaching or development.
- Poor role-modelling of what to do when times get tough.
- Reduced sense of personal responsibility—it's always someone else's fault.
- Low understanding of teamwork or what being a good team player entails.
- Having to make new coach-player relationships.

If you are a talented athlete then it can become difficult for talent ID personnel to keep track of you, and you may miss out on being seen when they're looking for players.

For the parents, changing teams incurs:

- Setting a poor example for your child.
- Loss of contact with parental group—increased isolation.
- Increased travel times (potentially).

Of course, there are times when it is necessary to move a child—particularly if the environment is physically or mentally unsafe. If this is the case, then it is your role as the parent to move vulnerable children out of this space and bring the actions to the attention of an authority. Sport should never be a place where a child feels threatened or bullied.

Activity 14—Pros and cons

Make a list of pros and cons about your child's current team or sport.

Pros	Cons

Be aware that as humans we are (unfortunately) seven times more likely to notice a negative than a positive. It's why the news outlets always put bad stuff up the front of the bulletins—it makes us stop and watch. As a society we like to whine, as it brings people together.

This exercise will make you stop and think about your child's environment and potentially realise that it isn't that bad at all. Look at the list you made and now revisit the 'pros' side—if you look hard, can you find some more positives?

If you are a person who notices the negatives too readily and lets the good stuff fly over your head, you need to do something about it. Life has too many bad things going on to not notice the good things, of which there are many. The key is to retrain your brain to notice the positives and we do this the same way we get better at anything … practice.

Every night, try writing down three good things that happened to you that day. Three things that you are thankful for. Don't write the same big thing each day like 'my family' or 'my health'. Instead, look for small things, like the person who held the door for you when you had your hands full, the cakes at morning tea a colleague took the trouble to make and the beautiful birds singing outside your house. Make these the story of your day instead of the bad stuff that we tend to dwell on. Studies from Harvard show that after twenty-one days of doing this our brains automatically starts to scan the world for positives. After forty-two days it showed reductions in stress and anxiety.[23]

This skill is enormously useful for sports parents. It helps them maintain perspective and not judge their kid's game on the three bad passes they made, but the ten good passes they made. The passes that otherwise would've gone unnoticed. It stops you stewing on the one bad thing the coach did and notice the other twenty good things he did.

Now go back and complete the last exercise again. See if there are some more positives you may have overlooked.

Action 1—Building resilience in your child

If you moved your child or are contemplating moving your child, you need to look at the full picture. Is it because the environment was unsafe, bullying was rampant, and the child was being emotionally or physically harmed? If so, then by all means remove the child from that environment. If it is simply because your child wasn't getting the position they wanted, they weren't one of the 'favourites', or the team lost more than they won, then you may have missed out on some valuable lessons.

The lesson I am talking about is *resilience*.

Resilience is an underrated life skill that is vital for sports people and non-sports people alike.

It's the ability to bounce back from setbacks, to push through tough times and deal with adversity—all things we inevitably encounter in life.

The recent 2016 Youth Resilience Survey found that across the country, 44 percent of students scored resilience levels described as 'good' to 'excellent', whilst 56 percent of students scored 'low' to 'fair'. Disturbingly, 30 percent believe they don't have an adult who cares about them and 43 percent reported being bullied at school in the last twelve months.[24]

You can see why resilience is such an important subject to discuss with your children.

Run or resilient

If your child is not getting the praise that you think they deserve or the position they covet then you have a choice. You can leave and find somewhere where things will be easier, or you can stay and deal with the adversity. I know which option teaches a greater lesson.

In 2015, all three of my kids were playing in elite squads run by the Football Federation of Victoria. You would think that this would be ample reason to be very proud of your kids. I can tell you Fiona and I certainly were proud. But it was what happened to our eldest, Ruby, that made us prouder than any sporting or educational achievement she had earned.

The squad she played in was made up of approximately thirty U/15–U/17 players from across the State. Each week they would select a team to play in the Women's Premier League Seniors' competition, and the rest would play in the WNPL Reserves' competition. Being an U/16 kid, she was expected to vie for senior selection while her younger sister Molly would spend most of the year in the Reserves. Ruby was coming off a very interrupted previous season which included stress fractures in her tibia and wasn't in the best shape of her life when the season started. She was told by the coach to get her fitness up and then she would be given an opportunity in the Seniors.

Well, the season progressed and instead of getting closer to senior selection, she was getting further away. Not a lot was said to her, but when she was being by passed week after week, she saw the writing on the wall. The situation was made even worse by her younger sister seeming to surpass her in the eyes of the coach, and it was Molly who was given the opportunities everyone expected Ruby to receive.

Come mid-season, Ruby was taken aside by the Head Coach and told that she would be one of two in the squad not to be selected to attend the National Training Centre Championships in Canberra. For a sixteen-year-old girl with high expectations, it was a kick in the guts and a big whack to her pride. A few snide remarks from some of the other girls did nothing to help the situation.

To her credit, instead of pleading her case she asked the coach for feedback on what she had to do to improve. 'It's your speed' was the answer. Okay, that's fair enough. She resisted the urge to make excuses such as the stress fractures and instead asked what she could do about it. Unfortunately the elite junior program in the State didn't have the resources to do *anything* about it, so they couldn't help.

I won't go on a rant here about the deficiencies of the so-called 'elite program', as the way Ruby reacted is the important aspect of this story. At this stage she could've done what five other kids did during the year—they packed up and went back to their local clubs. All had various reasons, but most of those reasons were to do with playing time, coach attention, non-specific training and selection issues.

I can't deny that joining the five others back in club land did go through Ruby's mind at some stage. The concept of being the big fish in the little pond does have its appeal. And when her sister was made captain of the U/15 state team it only accentuated the fact that she had missed out.

At this point I fully expected to get a tap on the shoulder from Ruby, sadly pointing out that she no longer wanted to make the two-hour round car trip to training three times a week, and that she had stacks of homework to do, and that the coach didn't like her, and the girls in the seniors are bitches, and that she isn't getting a fair go, et cetera, et cetera.

Instead I was taken quite by surprise. She said, 'Dad, can we get up at 6am three mornings a week and do some sprint work? I saw a quote that said "be so good that they can't ignore you" and that's what I want to do.'

Well, I know now what they mean when they say 'well up with pride'. I *welled up* so much I had tears coming out of my eyes.

Out of the two reactions she could've had, this was the one I'd hoped for, but being a teenage girl, I thought she would have the other. The path she was choosing was definitely not the easy path. It was paved with both physical and mental hurdles, but these did not deter her.

So, as much as I love my sleep-ins on cold Melbourne winter mornings, she got me out of bed three mornings a week, as well as weekends, to run up and down ramps that lead to the local beach. To do agility sprints, boxing, and the stairs we called the 'Black Rock buggers'—145 steps straight up.

Now you would probably say that all this story needs is a happy ending. One in which Ruby's perseverance pays off and she is finally selected for the WPL seniors, where she kicks the winning goal in the finals. Well, no, unfortunately she never made the senior team and despite playing very well in the Reserves, she was cut from the squad at season's end. Are we upset about that? No, not really. We had gotten so much more out of the program than we expected.

My message to the girls has always been that as long as you can walk away without any regrets, then you can hold your head high. Never say *I wish I had tried harder, I wish I had been fitter*, or *I wish I had listened to the coach more.* These are regrets you have to live with. If you do all the right things and you still miss out, then you can walk away satisfied and determined to be better next time. Despite doing everything in your power to succeed, sometimes things just don't work out.

This was one of those cases for Ruby. I could tell that although there was initial disappointment, she was comforted knowing that she gave it her all. I think she was evenly secretly happy with herself for how she reacted—it gave her an added confidence.

The lessons she learnt, as well as her newfound speed, would stand her in good stead for next season, wherever that may be. She also knew that her goal of playing College Soccer in the US was not diminished. In fact, the increased resilience will come in useful when she is 12,000 miles from home without her parents and sisters to lean on. As I said, I had never been prouder of one of my girls than I was of Ruby during the 2015 season.

To me this is a magnificent example of winning and recognition—things that we strive for so vehemently in sports—taking a backseat to life lessons. Who knows how many games either team won that season? And, basically, who cares? The life lessons learnt by my daughter are far more important than where her team finished on the ladder.

As parents and coaches we sometimes become so focused on the win/loss ratio and the level of recognition our kids are getting that we forget about the life lessons. I worry for the five girls who dropped out of the program. What lesson did they learn? That when things get tough you just move teams until you find somebody who recognises your talent and is willing to remove all obstacles from your path? How does that serve them when they enter the workforce and are overlooked for a promotion? Do they just pull up stumps and change careers? Or if that is too hard, do they simply hate going into work every day? The amount of people who hate facing their work each day is enormous. By allowing people to react to their situation rather than *choose* how they react, this number will continue to grow.

The key for parents is to take a step back. Avoid getting mired in the confusion that exists when your kids are facing obstacles. We know we have a natural instinct to protect them—it has been in us for millions of years and it is hard to let go of.

Often it means our first thought is to rail against authority, to approach the coach or the committee and complain about how my daughter is not having a perceived weakness addressed. To shout about how the program is insufficient, and that an elite program should cater for this type of occurrence. To be honest, I did ask the question of what they can do, but when the answer came back as 'nothing', then that's when the choices began. We could either keep complaining, run away, or do something about it ourselves. With Ruby's guidance we chose the latter, and because of this choice I now have a young girl who learnt so much more in season 2015 than she ever would have by being the star of her team.

Activity 15—Why move?

On the left-hand side, list the possible reasons why you would move your child to another team or coach.

On the right-hand side, list the benefits to your child by being resilient and staying put.

I have added in some examples to get your thinking started.

Why move?	**Why stay?**
My child isn't getting the position they want	Learn to work harder and take an opportunity when it comes
My child isn't getting the recognition they deserve	Learn to be so good the coach can't ignore you
Team morale isn't high	Learn to be a leader and drive morale and team spirit
You don't get along with the other parents	It's not about you
My child is not progressing fast enough	They are bottom age; going through a growth spurt; just not that talented yet; my expectations are too high; et cetera
My child won't get recognised here	Have faith that the cream will rise to the top

If your child is one of the 56 percent with low resilience, you may want to assess the suggested ways to build resilience.

- Create space at home for no technology, or limited technology. This promotes talking and involvement with the family, building relationships and trust.
- Increase praise and feedback to reinforce positive behaviours and attitudes. Don't be afraid to say 'well done' to them when they deserve it. When was the last time you genuinely did that?
- Praise effort and persistence rather than outcome. Ninety percent of your focus should be on what they are doing and not on what they are achieving.
- Keep your own levels of expectation in check.
- Place tips and strategies around the room to calm and relieve stress. With my kids, they must remember to breathe when things get a bit overwhelming. When my youngest experienced anxiety starting a new school, she would start each day by taking a piece of paper and writing down everything that was good about the school and the opportunities she would now have. The anxiety which made her throw up on the first two days was gone by the end of the week.
- Encourage participation in leisure and recreation activities to promote a healthy mind and body. Exercise releases endorphins which act as natural painkillers and make us feel good, so encourage them to stay active.
- Encourage young people to talk to a trusted adult. If they can't always talk to you, make sure they can talk to *someone*. Have a great relationship with your school and find out which teachers the kids relate to. You may have to call upon them if needed. Coaches who care for their players may be another resource.

Action 2—The dangers of 'generation get'

In today's culture, building a sense of 'team first' can be a challenge because of the continual focus on individual success. From an early age, people are encouraged to be the *star* of the team because it is the stars who receive the biggest rewards.

I recently saw a quote attributed to Cristiano Ronaldo, the Real Madrid champion, who has won multiple World Player of the Year titles. He said, 'I never tried to hide the fact that my only goal was to be the best.'[25] On the surface it is an admirable goal. He should be congratulated for having the courage to put himself forward in such a manner—some players want to be good but are afraid of the scrutiny and pressure that comes with being the best. And he should also be congratulated for working extremely hard to get where he is.

But to be honest, I would be far more excited about the quote if it came from a golfer, tennis player or even a darts player. The fact that it comes from a man who plays a team sport and whose 'only goal' is to be the best is concerning. Worse, it comes from a man who millions of young soccer players admire and want to emulate. That is downright troubling.

Ronaldo may think that he is contributing to his team by simply being the best player. Unfortunately, I get the sense that being World Player of the Year may be more important to him than a League Championship. I won't even mention running away from your teammates after you score a goal 'for your team'. At least in AFL we haven't gotten to that stage, and I doubt we ever will.

In many ways the idolisation of individuals in team sports diminishes the very fabric of what team sports is about—a group of people working *together* to overcome and defeat another group of people.

These days it's more like one group of talented individuals beating a group of less talented individuals. With comments like the above it is no wonder we have a generation of kids and parents focused on what they can *get* out of playing rather than what they can *give*. It doesn't have to be this way and we can change, provided we learn to refocus on the joys of contributing to a team, rather than on the joys of individual recognition.

As a parent, be conscious of how much you contribute to 'generation get' by talking only about positions you want your child to have, the pathway you want them to be on, or how much recognition you want them to receive. It is likely your child is picking up on these cues from you.

Later on, we will talk about modern sporting teams and how they are increasingly likely to insist on a team-first attitude from all its players—even traditional individual sports are going down the team-first path. Lleyton Hewitt, the coach of the Australian Men's Davis Cup team, openly states how he wants players to be part of the team and will pick team players over higher ranked individuals. Bernard Tomic is one notable player who strikes me as being more interested in seeing what he can get from the Davis Cup team than what he can give, and it's no wonder that he was asked to leave the team in 2018.[26]

The question for you as a parent is how much time do you spend talking to your child about what they can *give* to the team or the sport? How does that message compare to the amount of time you spend talking about what they can *get* out of the team or sport?

If it isn't 75 percent in favour of what they can give, then you have some adjustments to make.

Turning the tide

The question is *what can we do about it?* How can we change mindsets, especially in team sports, so that kids are more concerned about the team rather than their own position in it?

Start by asking the kids one simple question—what are you going to *give* to the team? This may stump many of them, as all they will have concentrated on is what can they *get* from the team.

Hopefully you will hear answers like:

- My leadership
- My skills
- My fitness
- My enthusiasm
- My encouragement
- My competitiveness
- My humour
- My best effort
- My selflessness
- My commitment
- My discipline.

Once they become clear on these points, they will hopefully be less focused on individual esteem and more focused on collective gain. You may need to explain the notion of teamwork a little further and why people play a team sport, as they have more than likely come to focus on the negatives of being in a team, such as having to share the spotlight. Getting a young athlete out of the 'poor me', self-victimising mindset can be a nightmare once it has been ingrained in them. And if your child plays an individual sport, I guarantee they will be part of a team one day—hopefully an Olympic Team.

Therefore it is best to teach them what it means to be a team player from an early age.

Importantly, being a team player is within your control, whilst the coach you have is often not within your control. This is another key point all young athletes need to learn: The best athletes only concern themselves with what is in their control. They don't worry about things outside of their control, like other people's opinions.

When you have a group of people who are willing to give rather than get, you will have a great team.

I suggest Ronaldo learns from the following men who have a good grasp on what being a member of a team means:

'Respect your fellow human being, treat them fairly, disagree with them honestly, enjoy their friendship, explore your thoughts about one another candidly, work together for a common goal and help one another achieve it.'—Bill Bradley, basketballer.[27]

'Getting good players is easy. Getting them to play together is the hard part.'—Casey Stengel, baseballer.[28]

'It is amazing what can be accomplished when nobody cares about who gets the credit.'—Robert Yates, politician.[29]

Finally, a reminder: They don't have twenty-year reunions for people who win individual awards. Only successful *teams* celebrate their achievements long term.

Activity 16—What can you give?

Start your child's journey from being part of 'generation get' to 'generation give'. Have them list all the things they can *get* from the team, squad or club they belong to. Then have them list the things they can *give* to the team, squad or sport.

Things I can *get* from this team/sport	**Things I can *give* to this team/sport**

Here are some tips for your kids on what they can do to become givers, and better team players:

- Pick up water bottles, bibs, practice balls, et cetera.
- Organise a team get-together.
- Practice hard every session.
- Help others with extra training to develop their skills.
- Cheer from the sidelines or bench.
- Reinforce and live the team rules.
- Be vocal in meetings.
- Display a positive, confident attitude.
- Ask what you can do to help the team improve.
- Ask for guidance on how *you* can improve.
- Get there early, leave late.
- Offer to review games.
- Never miss a training.
- Show good sportsmanship.
- Smile and be friendly.
- Publicly acknowledge others' good fortune or performance.
- Only speak of the positives and address the negatives with the coach in private.
- Be sefless.
- Encourage others, say 'well done, great job'.

I guarantee that if your kids do these actions, they will receive positives in return. I am not a religious person, but I do believe in sporting karma. Good things happen to good people. Which is why the team with the highest winning percentage in world sport, the New Zealand All Blacks—a Rugby Union team—have as one of their key pillars that 'better men make better All Blacks'. If it comes down to a choice between a great player with a poor attitude and a good player with a great attitude, they will always choose the latter. For this person will *give* their all for the team; they will make the people around them better; and, importantly, uphold the traditions, culture, and legacy the All Blacks have worked so hard to build. Because world sport is filled with copycats, you can expect a whole raft of sports to adopt these principles. We have seen it with the Sydney Swans adopting a similar but cruder 'no dickheads policy' when it comes to choosing new players.

After completing the exercise you may just find that you and your child develop an attitude that will stand you both in good stead for many seasons to come. And, importantly, your child may develop a positive reputation—something more important than their level of skill—that will see them progress in their sport and be a highly sought-after team player. Certainly good enough to pass the 'no dickheads policy', at least.

Chapter 6—Summary

If you're a parent who constantly needs your kid to be the centre of the court, pitch, or field, then you have an issue.

Quite often, parents like this will bounce their child from team to team every season, seeking out the validation, development and esteem they believe their child deserves. In 90 percent of cases, it is not the child making this decision, but their overbearing sports parent.

Selection at higher levels involves far more than having the skills to play. There is a lot of talent to go around these days, so a coach will also be on the lookout for good people, good teammates, and good role models. If it comes down to a choice between a litigious person who runs to court when they don't get their own way or a selfless team player, the latter will almost always prevail.

Build resilience

Moving your child out of a team when they aren't getting the praise you think they deserve or playing the position they covet deprives them of an important lesson in *resilience.*

Of course, there are times when it is necessary to move a child. If the environment is unsafe; mentally, emotionally or physically; then it is the parent's duty to take their child out of that space. (And report the situation where appropriate.)

But if your child leaves the team for one of the aforementioned issues, what message does that send them? That when things get tough you just move teams until you find somebody who recognises your talent and is willing to remove all obstacles from your path?

The key for parents is to take a step back. Avoid getting mired in the confusion that exists when your kids are facing obstacles.

Generation get

In today's culture, building a sense of 'team first' can be a challenge because of the continual focus on individual success.

Teach your child to be a team player by asking them one simple question: what are you going to *give* to the team? Until now, they've probably been more focused on what they can *get* from the team.

When you have a group of people willing to give rather than get, you will have a team.

If you need help with actual actions, I have provided a little cheat sheet below. Sometimes it's about what you *don't* do as much as what you do.

- Stop whining to anyone who will listen.
- Stop undermining the coach every chance you get.
- Cheer from the sidelines.
- Pick up water bottles, bibs, practice balls, et cetera.
- Organise a team get-together.
- Practice harder.
- Help others with extra training to develop their skills.
- Reinforce the team rules or mission statement.
- Be vocal in meetings.
- Display a positive attitude.
- Ask what you can do to improve.
- Ask for guidance on how to improve.
- Offer to review games.

Chapter 7

Nine tips to help you be a Best and Fairest Sports Parent

The first section of this book involved a lot of self-reflection and some actions you can take to improve your attitudes. For those of you who came through the assessment in good shape, there will still be areas where you can improve. The following pages will outline some quick wins you can have on your road to being a Best and Fairest Sports Parent. Many of them will entail minor adjustments on your behalf but I guarantee they will lead to major changes in both the way your child approaches their sport and, most importantly, how they approach you—the most important person in their lives right now.

1. Note the small things they do in a game.

Pulling off the game-winning hit or kicking the miraculous goal is every kid's dream, but in reality it rarely happens. If you are a parent waiting for the big moment before you get excited, it will only end in disappointment.

One way to avoid this is to take note of all the small things your child does in a game. Make that your focus on these rather than looking for the game winner.

It's essential for kids to know that you're watching and paying attention to their efforts. They will appreciate it and realise that they don't have to pull off the 'miracle play' in order to get some praise. You will often find kids going outside team rules or attempting things that they aren't capable of just to get some attention. It is a nightmare scenario for coaches, teammates, and for you, as it signals a damaged relationship.

In my opinion, nothing is sadder than when a child does something they are happy with or proud of in competition, then glances across to where their parents are sitting, and they see their mum or dad on the phone or deep in conversation with the other parents. You can almost see their little heart break. If you are unsure whether you fit into this category, think back to a time when your child has asked you if you saw something they did in the game. Often, they'll ask you on the drive home. At the time, did you respond with, 'No, I missed it'? If you did, you may have gotten a response like, 'I don't know why you bother coming if you're not gonna watch.' Or worst still, silence, as they realise that they failed to impress the person they want to impress the most.

You don't have to be able to recall every moment of the game, but if you can redeem yourself by saying, 'No, I missed that one, but I did see that forehand winner on the run—that was great', then you will still most likely have a happy child.

If you can't attend the games in person, make sure you ask how they played—not just who won or lost. It will help if you know enough about the game to ask if they did some of the small things well, such as:

- Did you make any tackles?
- How was your first touch?
- How was your backhand today?
- Did anything funny happen today?
- What was the best part about playing?

My girls use to laugh at their mother, who—before they started playing soccer—had absolutely no idea about the game. Understanding the offside rule was akin to learning algebra to her, but because she made it her business to take note of what was happening, to learn the game, she has built up a bank of knowledge that is quite impressive. Over time she has earned the right to make suggestions to the girls, who listen to what she has to say. Whilst their dad has a sporting background, which comes with a degree of credibility in their eyes, it has been useful for the girls to be able to discuss things with their mum, too. Unfortunately, dads don't always have the right tact when dealing with young girls. We tend to go straight into solution mode, which isn't always what they want to hear. A mum however will have the ability to hear a young girl out, wait for the right time and *then* offer a solution. A mum who knows the game *and* has this ability can be a powerful ally to any young sports girl. It's also a reason why coach education should be targeting women and giving them more opportunities to coach.

Again, this is where it is important to know which aspects of the game your child is personally working on. If you know they are working on tackling, then ask about it, and give them a pump up when they say they did a couple of rippers.

All of this will take the anxiety out of winning, losing and having to be the star of the game in order to get some attention. It doesn't take much effort on your behalf but will make a big difference to your child. After all, will your business go under, or Facebook or the newspaper cease existing in the time it takes to watch an U/12 tennis match on a Saturday morning?

2. Display positive body language.

When your kid looks over at you, it may not be enough for them just to see you watching—why not give them a nod, a wink or thumbs up? When you do, I guarantee you will physically see their confidence and self-belief lift. This is far better than seeing a grumpy parent with their arms folded or someone who is constantly on their phone.

I have seen and heard so many stories of children who have gone so far as to ban their parents from attending games because of the pressure they put on their kids. The parent will say, 'But I don't say anything, I just stand there.' What they don't realise is that their body language speaks volumes. Especially when a child is looking for approval, they will read into any gesture that signals non-approval. As frustrated as you are on the inside, you can't let it show on the outside; that is the coach's job. Pacing back and forth, over-exaggerated reactions to misses and successes all send signals to the kids that might disrupt their ideal mental state in a game. I don't know of many kids who can maintain high levels of confidence after they make a mistake when out of the corner of their eye, they see you throwing your head back in desperation.

The key is not to *react* to the situation. Reacting connotes instant action—it's almost reflexive. For example, when you see a bad miss and react by groaning audibly. Far better is to *respond* to the action by choosing the most appropriate response. As much as you might want to collapse into despair, think first about what that would do to the child. They will probably be feeling the pain of that miss more than you, so why would you want to make them feel worse? You can be damn sure they didn't make the mistake on purpose.

Think about what sort of mindset your child will need to be in the next time that situation arises. If it's a confident one, then a thumbs up and a smile is more likely to achieve that than a groan and a buried head. You may ask yourself *why* your child is really playing poorly, or wonder how to respond when you can't accept how they let themselves and the team down. It's a good question. First of all you must understand why your child is not performing well. Is it because they are trying too hard, maybe playing against really good opposition, or could they be having a little crisis with their confidence? If this is the case, then standing there with a disgusted look on your face will do no good at all.

If it is because your child is just not giving the required level of effort—that they are taking things too easy or skylarking—then speak to them about it. They need to know that this behaviour is inappropriate. A post-game question such as, 'Did you take them a little easy today?' said in a non-judgmental, non-angry way is more likely to elicit an honest response of, 'Yeah, I did' from the child. If they think you are mad at them, then they are more likely to avoid the truth and bluff their way out of it. No child wants to make an angry parent even angrier by admitting to doing something wrong. Their first instinct will be to placate the angry parent, which is why you are much more likely to get an honest review of the performance if you keep your cool. Anger and disappointment will only cloud the message.

The lines of communication between you and your child must be healthy enough that you can bring up concepts like effort or showing off and not have the conversation dissolve into a game of blame, denial and justification. If the child is taking it too easy, then it is the coach's responsibility to address that. If you don't think the coach will do that, then make an appointment to talk about it later in the week.

If your child is genuinely fatigued, not sleeping well, or is even being bullied by other kids in the team, then they are far less likely to bring this up to an angry parent. And this is a huge problem. Left unchecked, these issues can be the catalyst to the child walking away from the sport or, worse, walking away from you. Remember; your child's sport is not about you or how *you* feel about it. It is all about them. You have to be the adult and respond to situations so that your child receives the best outcome, not react in a way that makes *you* feel better.

3. Before the game, fill them with belief.

Reinforce the good aspects of your child's team and their abilities. Don't fill them with fear by spending twenty minutes talking about how outstanding the other team is. How often have you heard parents try to pump their kids up by saying, 'Boy this other team is rough, they beat the top team last week, you guys are in for a really tough one today'? Whilst we have all made comments like this, think about what it can potentially do a child's pre-game mental state. Maybe we're trying to fire them up, it is more likely to have the opposite effect—they become less likely to take risks and more likely to play within themselves. They can become scared to try things, and self-doubt replaces confidence.

A far better system is to point out the quality of the opposition and then focus on what the children need to do to overcome the quality opponent. Talk about the good points of their play and the actual tangible actions they will have to undertake on the field. Think of the child's mindset at the start of the game—you don't want them to be thinking, *Oh no, this team is tough, we will probably get smashed today.* Instead, you want them to think, *I'm going to use my skills and do all the team things today, and we'll show these guys what a good team is.*

Talking about the other team often just helps the parent's mindset and makes them feel good. They think they have done their bit to focus the kids, when in reality, the parent's mindset is completely inconsequential to the game. The only important thing is what goes through the *child's* head before and after kick-off or the first bounce or whistle. After all, they are the ones in the arena.

This is where it is best to take heed from one of Theodore Roosevelt's famous quote:

> 'It is not the critic who counts; not the man who points out how the strong man stumbles, or where the doer of deeds could have done them better. The credit belongs to the man who is actually in the arena, whose face is marred by dust and sweat and blood; who strives valiantly; who errs, who comes short again and again, because there is no effort without error and shortcoming; but who does actually strive to do the deeds; who knows great enthusiasms, the great devotions; who spends himself in a worthy cause; who at the best knows in the end the triumph of high achievement, and who at the worst, if he fails, at least fails while daring greatly, so that his place shall never be with those cold and timid souls who neither know victory nor defeat.'[30]

4. Model good sportsmanship.

No matter what the end score, say 'well done' to the opposition and umpires when they walk past. Where will a child get a better role model for sportsmanship than their parents? Maybe a coach and yes, a coach is vitally important, but the coach is with the child for maybe three hours a week, maybe twenty weeks of the year. Apart from when your child is asleep or at school, they are usually with you. This is why *you* have the power to influence a child's level of sportsmanship the most.

Whenever you have the chance, point out good examples of sportsmanship and also poor examples. Let them know how much you respect and admire the good sports of the world. There are plenty of them out there and they come from all walks of life. It may be the jockey beaten by a nose in the Melbourne Cup who pats the winning jockey on the back straight after they pass the post, or the singer on *Australia's Got Talent* who immediately and genuinely hugs the winner despite feeling internally devastated. There are examples all over the world of good and bad sportsmanship and it's your role as parents to find them and point them out—not to mention encourage your children to seek out more examples on their own.

This is one reason why I am not necessarily a fan of the no-scoreboard trend in junior sport. If a coach and their parent group are worth their salt, they will teach the children how to lose and just as importantly how to win with grace. If nobody ever wins or loses, how do you impart those lessons?

As tough as this may be, you have to extend that sportsmanship to the referees and officials of the sport. I have at times lapsed in this area as I have allowed the emotions of competition to cloud my better judgment. On every occasion I had the guilts driving home and pledged to rein myself in. Fortunately I have managed to do so and enjoy the game far better because of it. It's amazing what a few stints as linesperson in a game of soccer will do to your concept of how hard the job is. I suggest you take the opportunity to put yourself in the ump's shoes from time to time if you can. The good ones make it look easy but that's only because they are the good ones.

5. Cheer.

Cheer, but don't get carried away (and never cheer the opposition's mistakes). Also cheer for the other kids in the team, not just yours. This is where the ability to put yourself in other people's shoes comes in handy. Just think how you would feel if your child made an error and the opposition parent group all started cheering. I dare say there would be some anger going around. And let's not forget how your child would feel. The old saying of 'do unto others' is pertinent here.

Also think about how good you feel when other parents say 'well done' to your kids. Why not return the favour occasionally?

As for the over-the-top cheering, just be wary of your volume and what you yell. Your child will have a coach, so let them coach and give instructions, but there is nothing wrong with congratulating or celebrating success. Sport is first and foremost supposed to be fun; someone saying 'well done' is one of the things that makes playing sport fun. Where is the fun for a kid who does something well and is met with silence? I don't subscribe to the 'parents should be seen and not heard' doctrine. This edict normally comes from overly possessive coaches who are insecure and believe their message may be diluted by a bit of encouragement from the parent group. There is a middle ground that sits between over-the-top and silence. In the middle ground sits encouragement, congratulations and sportsmanship. Outside it sits abuse, angst, silence, sarcasm, chiding, excessive noise and an aggressive demeanour. A good test for knowing where you stand is taking note of how many people choose to sit on the other side of the stadium or field from you. If you are alone, it is generally for a reason.

An interesting way to look at your performance on the sidelines is to compare it to the grandparents who come to watch. Most kids love their grandparents coming to watch because they know that they won't be judging them and are there purely because they love watching them play. Win, lose or draw, they smile and hug their grandkids as soon as they come off the field. Kids pick up on this and will often say, 'I love it when Grandma and Grandpa come and watch us play.'

Do they say the same about you? At your next game try thinking like a grandparent—don't be obsessed with the score or the performance. Just enjoy watching them play and enjoy themselves.

6. Be patient.

Understand that even the world's best players make ridiculous clangers … and so will your child.

Remember the exercise I asked you to do in Chapter 1, Action 1 when watching professional sport? Whatever sport your child plays, sit down and analyse a professional game played by full-time professionals. Count how many errors they make, how many times they turn the ball over, miss a shot, drop a mark or have bad first touch. I guarantee you will be surprised. They happen far more regularly than the miraculous shot or goal—the stuff that sticks in our mind. When you realise how often the full-time pros make mistakes, maybe you'll go a little easier on your twelve-year-old who doesn't always hit their target. If you want to, you can go one step further and get out there and have a go yourself. I know of a junior soccer coach and a junior tennis coach who insist on all the parents playing a pre-season game just to remind them of how hard the games are to play, and that mistakes are part of the experience.

I often laugh when I sit next to ex-footballers who, after a few years out of the game, believe that the game is somehow easy to play. Sure you can see all the gaps in the play from way up in the stands, but could you still see them if you were down there getting thumped into the ground by an opponent in front of 30,000 people? No, you couldn't, so sit back and try to remember how hard sport can be.

Mistakes will happen in all games at all levels; even the most basic of mistakes. Teach your child that mistakes are part of the game and a game with no mistakes is impossible. The most important thing is what you do *after* you make the mistake. Do you stand and sulk, or try to win the ball back, or go for that serve again? That is often the true test of elite sportspeople—not how many mistakes they make, but how they react after making them. The example you set as a parent will go a long way to determining which attitude your child generates.

The other end of the spectrum is a child who is too afraid to make mistakes, so they never try anything in a game. I had the feeling one of my daughters was feeling this way, as no matter how often I implored her to try things in a game, she was always reluctant. Some kids just don't want to look silly or be seen to have a big head by trying things like step overs in soccer or three-pointers in basketball. It was her personality along with my praise of the steady players in the team; the ones who did all of the team things well; that made her reluctant to make a mistake. In hindsight, my praising of the 'steady players' led her to think that taking risks was not the thing to do. Simply encouraging her to take the game on was not enough to change her mindset. A sit-down talk discussing the need to make mistakes in order to grow and learn helped, along with a conscious effort on my part to reward effort and not outcome.

Girls especially are more likely to need this talk. Many young girls are almost pre-programmed to avoid embarrassing situations. Doing a step over on a soccer pitch in front of teammates, parents, referees and spectators and falling on your butt is certainly embarrassing. When coaching girls, you must go out of your way to celebrate mistakes, count them and encourage them, as it will take this additional effort to eradicate the pre-programming. There are exceptions to each rule and some girls will try the extraordinary or not be afraid to make a mistake. Think about it—are they the best players in the team? They probably are, aren't they? Funny that.

It is amazing what kids can understand. If you make their lack of risk-taking your fault and not theirs, they will be fell far better about it.

7. Greet them with a smile.

Start with a smile and a hug before you launch into any post-game analysis. There is a lot of evidence that the ride home in the car after the game is the most important time in the child athlete's development.

So much can be gained and lost in those post-game interactions. In previous chapters, we discussed the danger of imposing your thoughts, feelings and identity onto your child. A good way to avoid falling into this trap is to smile and hug. This will prevent you from saying things you shouldn't and cast aside any apprehensions the child may have after a poor performance. As much as you want to ask what happened or dissect every element of the game ... don't. Even if you're feeling angry on the inside, don't let it show.

The key is to develop a relationship with the child whereby, after they have calmed down from the disappointment of losing, *they* will broach the subject of the game. Then, when they have opened the door to that conversation, your job is to ask questions rather than bombard them with tips. *What do you think happened out there today? What did you do well? What do you think you can improve on?* If they don't have answers, then you can then fill in the gaps in a helpful and non-judgmental fashion.

It's important to play the long game here and not try to fix everything in one discussion. If you are experienced enough to know what your child should be working on, pick the most pertinent skill and leave it at that. The child will not be able to remember all five things they need to improve—all they will hear is, 'Boy, you did a lot of things wrong.' The long game means taking little steps, getting one thing right, and then working on the next. If you do this over the course of the season, you will improve, but if you try to work on everything in the short-term, you will more than likely destroy your child's confidence and enjoyment of the game.

If you are unsure about which skill is the most pertinent, go and ask the coach. If they say, 'I am trying to get them to improve their non-dominant side', then there's your opening—*how did you go with your left foot today?* If they did one kick well, then praise them for that. If they mucked them all up, then encourage them to keep trying and practicing.

If you're lucky enough for them to come to you for advice, give them one piece at a time. Don't take the opportunity to point out ten things they can do better. Just give them your best one and they will be far more likely to return for more.

8. Praise appropriately.

Your child will not be outstanding in every game—no-one is. When they have a down game, acknowledge it with a smile and a cuddle and encourage them to get straight back on the horse. Praising your child inappropriately; telling them they will win *X Factor* when they are clearly tone-deaf; does no-one any good. If your child shows no talent at a particular skill, praise the effort, but don't unrealistically praise the results. Be genuine and drop the meaningless flattery. Smart kids can see through the falsity and it lessens the impact when they do something truly praiseworthy.

If your child performs well below their capability, don't say they were fantastic and go overboard to buck them up. You can tell them that they were below their best. Importantly, keep things in perspective and discuss how even champion players don't always have great games. But what they *do* is honestly analyse why they may not have been great. Was it because they didn't get enough sleep before the game? Maybe they didn't eat right, or maybe that little niggle of an injury needs some rest. Or maybe they just took their opponent a little too easy today.

Champions look at what *they* did or didn't do and never fall into patterns of blame, such as 'the coach put me in the wrong spot', or 'the balls were flat', or 'the referee was against me'. That sort of discussion never reaches a solution and only ever concerns itself with the past. Champions take personal responsibility for their performance, so make sure your child does the same. Your demeanour and gentle questioning will help them achieve this.

On the other hand, it's amazing how many parents are afraid to say 'well done' when their kid deserves it. Young kids especially measure their worth and achievement by what *you* think. Don't go overboard, but don't miss an opportunity either.

Again, this is where it is important to know what your child is trying to work on—where they want to improve—so you can reinforce their effort by recognising when they *do* improve. If you don't know, then you will fall into the trap of praise when they win and no praise when they don't.

And be careful about how much you post on social media about your child. I know it is tempting to put every good result up on Facebook, but put yourself in your child's shoes. Don't embarrass them, and remember their feelings come before your need to let the world know how good of an athlete your child is. Instead, be selective and choose what is most worthy of reporting online. Ask yourself whether you are posting the story because you are proud of your child's performance, or because you want people to know how good *your* kid is—is it more about you or the child?

9. Be helpful and support their passion.

Be a support rather than a coach, as they probably already have a coach. Remember that they don't have to be the best at what they do—they just have to enjoy what they do. Whether it is sport, art, music, dance, technology, education, Scouts, it doesn't matter. You may not like watching cricket for hours on a Saturday but if it means a confident, happy child, suck it up. Every kid will find something they enjoy. When they have fun, they will do it more often (practice), get better at it (improve) and with each achievement they will gain confidence. Other benefits include the ability to recognise their strengths; accept or strengthen their weaknesses; handle defeat; expand their circle of friends; and learn teamwork. Another confidence-boosting bonus: they stay fit and learn to respect their bodies. With the obesity epidemic among children, this is important, even if your child doesn't wish to pursue organised sports.

Supporting their passion does not mean buying the most expensive equipment or paying for private coaching. We covered this in Chapter 4. Supporting their passion means making sure they enjoy their sport, making sure you're taking an interest in their sport, and not falling into the behaviours of an under-involved parent. These behaviours can include:

- You take no interest in your child's sport.
- You see sport as babysitting, which gets your kid out of your hair for several hours a week.
- You don't hold your child responsible for their bad behaviour.
- You don't recognise the benefits sport can provide your child.
- You don't reinforce the positive lessons and learnings.
- Not being present at games, or when you do attend, you sit in the car and read a book. If you are there, be there!
- You never discuss your child's participation, ups, downs, likes or dislikes.
- You have no idea who the coach is and what example they are setting for your child.
- You don't help to make sport fun.
- You won't read books like this.

Research also tells us that when teachers and parents work together, the child does better at school. The same applies to sports when coaches and parents work together. Where possible, strike up a positive relationship with the coach. Ask how you can help and volunteer for roles such as linesperson, timekeeper, washing the singlets, et cetera. When you have a positive relationship with the coach you will in a better position to chat with them should a problem arise.

At the end of the day you have to ask yourself, what is more important? My child realising their full sporting potential, or our parent-child relationship?

If you answered either one you are wrong.

It *is* possible for a child to reach their full potential *and* maintain a healthy, loving and lasting relationship with their parents.

You don't have to sacrifice one for the other!

You can have it all, and you should aim to have it all. It just takes work, concentration and a great degree of self-awareness and even self-restraint. At times you will be frustrated, angry, defensive and downright mad. These are the emotions of life. The key is to choose the right emotion for the right circumstance and, as a parent, choose the one that brings about the right outcome for your kid. That's what making sacrifices for our kids means.

Epilogue

By now you are feeling one of two ways about yourself. You are either feeling down because you recognise a lot of these negative parenting traits in yourself … or you are feeling excited about the things you have learned and are eager to put them into practice. May I suggest you lean towards the latter and enjoy your kids formative sporting years?

But let me caution you, as the issues don't disappear when your kids reach adulthood.

One of my favourite and most rewarding roles I have ever occupied is Head Coach of the Western Bulldogs AFLW team. The Bulldogs participate in the National Australian Football League Women's Competition. The age group of the thirty listed players comprises of eighteen to thirty-four years olds, and is best described as semi-professional. Some players earn enough to be full-time professionals while others supplement their football income through other vocations.

When choosing players to come into our team, we always meet with the player and—where possible—their parents, as we like to think we draft the whole package.

Each season we change (on average) five players from the list of thirty. At this elite level it is rare that the choice between two players is obvious, especially when drafting young talent. We have to make value judgments in order to prefer one player over another.

If a player's parents throw up too may red flags, then the choice becomes a lot easier. The fact is, when money and fame are a part of the scene, any crack can quickly widen. I suggest you do the work now so that you too can handle the added pressure that money and fame add to the adult sporting equation.

The good news is that if your son or daughter ends up at a great club (like the Bulldogs) the organisation should make things easy for you. I will tell you a story of how, as a coach and playing group, we make things easy for parents.

When I first took over as coach, we won our practice matches, we won our first game, and everything was looking really rosy. Our second in-season game, we lost against our arch enemy, the Melbourne Demons. In the meeting room after the game I could see the question on the players' faces—how was this new coach going to handle losing? Was he going to yell, was he going to sulk, be disappointed, or gloss over it?

I could sense their confusion, so I wrote 'TLC' in large letters on the whiteboard and asked the players what they thought it stood for.

Some players thought they knew but were too unsure to speak up. Others were thinking, *hang on, Tender, Loving Care? This guy is older than my dad—I don't really want that from him.*

Finally, I put them out of their misery. I said, 'TLC is how we will handle any setback or perceived failure as long as I am your coach.'

The T stands for 'temporary'. The way you are feeling after a loss; dejected, sad, frustrated; will not last forever. It's important to understand that these feelings are temporary. You will get over them and start to feel like your old self again. When you understand this, it gives you the power to decide how long you feel the negative thoughts for.

As a team, we agreed that by the time the players do their cool-down, have a shower and collect their belongings ... that is long enough. No good will be served by continuing to feel dejected into the night or the coming days. So we decided that when they walk out of the rooms, it is with a smile on their face, shoulders back and head held high.

The L stands for 'localised'. Players and athletes tend to catastrophise things after poor performances. We need to understand that losing a game of football doesn't make the participants bad daughters, bad partners, bad friends, bad colleagues, bad (insert roles you play in life). Losing a game should not affect all the other important positions you hold in life. At the Bulldogs, we localise the disappointment to football *only* and not let it affect the other parts of our lives.

The C stands for 'control'. This is where we direct all our attention toward the things that we can control. We make a list of them, which may include how we recover, how we honestly review the game, and how hard we train during the week. This does not guarantee a different result the following week, but it absolutely gives us a better chance of winning than if we were to stew on the result or blame others for the loss.

When a player walks out after practicing TLC, her parents are instantly relieved. They just want their daughter to be happy and when they see her smile and know that she is okay, then they can relax, too.

So, at the Bulldogs, our players play a big role in helping their parents and family to choose the right reactions to winning and losing.

Whenever I get a chance to talk to the parent group at the Bulldogs, I always throw in a reminder about the TLC. It is important that the parents know what we are working on and how the process works.

There will still be members of the parent group, media and supporters who think that a person with a smile on their face doesn't care about the result. They want us to be as heartbroken as they are about losing a game. Rest assured, we care ... a lot. We just know that sulking about the result will not help us get a different result next week.

Athletes have a lot going through their minds and if the parent group can help the players work through TLC, then several things occur: the player recovers and moves on a lot faster; the relationship between player and parent is increased, as no-one is walking around on eggshells; and my job as coach becomes far easier.

If you would like to be a Best and Fairest Sports Parent, may I suggest that TLC (temporary, localised, control) combined with the original meaning of TLC (tender, loving care) is a wonderful place to start.

My aim as a sports dad

My youngest daughter Alice plays in a rival AFLW team (my old team, the Saints). Because of my role coaching a rival team, I need to be very aware of which hat I put on—coach hat or dad hat. I have learnt that it is vital that I put my 'dad hat' on when she is playing. If I put the wrong one on, bad things can occur.

If she walks out dejected after a loss, my natural instincts kick in and I try to make everything better. In my efforts to make her feel better I may inadvertently say things that are contradictory to what the coach's message was. For instance, in an effort to deflect blame for the loss, I may observe that it was the midfield's fault for letting the ball come in too quickly, when in fact the coach was happy with them and upset with the defense. This observation serves only to confuse the player.

But when she walks out and I can see she is practicing TLC, I can relax my natural tendency to make things alright for her and give her space to work through the game herself, in her own time. My need to make things okay is reduced, as is my desire to offer coaching tips. I can see that she is okay. She knows that when she is ready to talk or ask for advice, I am there … but only in her own time. Our rule is that she has to ask for help or advice and I am not to offer it unsolicited. She already has a raft of coaches to help her be a better footballer.

If you see me at a game, I will often have the same baseball hat on. This is my 'dad hat' and is a personal reminder, or trigger, that I don't have my 'coaching hat' on today. I am there to support my daughter and to love her—no matter whether she wins, loses, is the best or worst player on that team.

My ultimate dream is to sit back one day, when we are both too old to play or coach and reminisce about the wonderful times and experiences we shared on and off the sporting field.

I hope through the tips and techniques we have discussed in the book that you and your children can do the same.

Endnotes

1 'French "tennis drugs" trial opens,' BBC News Europe, published March 2003, *http://news.bbc.co.uk/1/hi/world/europe/4762458.stm.*

2 LZ Granderson, 'Jennifer Capriati still battling,' ESPN, published July 14, 2012, *https://www.espn.com/tennis/story/_/id/8163920/jennifer-capriati-battling.*

3 'Tennis' Lucic Says Dad Is Abusive,' Associated Press, published August 1998, *https://apnews.com/article/cc31510d922868643677f2ae87a894e3.*

4 Cory Turner, 'When Kids Start Playing To Win,' NPR Ed, published August 5, 2014, *https://www.npr.org/sections/ed/2014/08/05/331412567/when-kids-start-playing-to-win.*

5 Amanda J Visek, et al. 'The fun integration theory: toward sustaining children and adolescents sport participation,' Journal of physical activity & health 12, no. 3 (2015): 424-33. *doi:10.1123/jpah.2013-0180.*

6 *Ibid.*

7 Julianna W. Miner, 'Why 70 percent of kids quit sports by age 13,' The Washington Post, published 1 July, 2016, *https://www.washingtonpost.com/news/parenting/wp/2016/06/01/why-70-percent-of-kids-quit-sports-by-age-13/.*

8 Victor Frankl, Man's Search for Ultimate Meaning (US: Basic Books, revised ed. 2000).

9 *Ibid.*

10 'USU Researchers: High Sport Spending doesn't Equal High Enjoyment,' Utah State Today, published April 2014, *https://www.usu.edu/today/story/usu-researchers-high-sport-spending-doesnt-equal-high-enjoyment.*

11 'TD Ameritrade Survey: Parents Prioritize Kids' Sports Spending Over Retirement Planning,' TD Ameritrade, published July 2016, *https://www.businesswire.com/news/home/20160801005136/en/Parents-of-Elite-Athletes-Score-Big-in-Commitment-to-Kids-Yet-Sideline-Financial-Goals.*

12 'How Likely Is It, Really, That Your Athletic Kid Will Turn Pro?' NPR, Robert Wood Foundation & Harvard T.H. Chan School of Public Health, published September 2015, *https://www.npr.org/sections/health-shots/2015/09/04/432795481/how-likely-is-it-really-that-your-athletic-kid-will-turn-pro.*

13 *Ibid.*

14 David Epstein, *The Sports Gene: Inside The Science of Extraordinary Athletic Performance* (US: Portfolio, 2014).

15 'Benefits – Why Sports Participation for Girls and Women,' Women's Sports Foundation, published August 2016, *https://www.womenssportsfoundation.org/advocacy/benefits-sports-participation-girls-women/.*

16 Utah State Today, supra endnote 10.

17 Amanda J Visek, et al, *supra endnote 5.*

18 Leisel J Jones & Felicity McLean, *Body Lengths* (Melbourne: Black Inc. Books, 2017).

19 Carol S Dweck, *Mindset: The New Psychology of Success* (US: Ballantine Books, 2007)

20 'Father sues his son's high school for $40 million when the 16-year-old was cut from his track team,' Daily Mail UK, published May 2013, *https://www.dailymail.co.uk/news/article-2331691/Father-sues-sons-high-school-40million-16-year-old-cut-track-team.html.*

21 Ben Rohrbach, 'Texas lacrosse dad files racketeering charges against coach who sat his son,' Yahoo! Sports, published April 2014, *https://sports.yahoo.com/blogs/highschool-prep-rally/texas-lacrosse-dad-files-racketeering-charges-against-coach-who-sat-his-son-162623616.html#:~:text=Attorney%20William%20Munck%20has%20filed,for%20his%20high%20school%20team.*

22 Justin Jouvenal, 'Teen volleyball player takes her dispute to another kind of court,' The Washington Post, published March 2015, *https://www.washingtonpost.com/local/crime/teen-volleyball-player-takes-her-dispute-to-another-kind-of-court/2015/03/31/e72fb174-c8f0-11e4-b2a1-bed1aaea2816_story.html.*

23 Shawn Achor, 'Is happiness the secret of success?' CNN Opinion, published March 2021, *https://edition.cnn.com/2012/03/19/opinion/happiness-success-achor/index.html.*

24 'Resilience Survey,' Resilient Youth Australia, published 2016, *https://resilientyouth.org/survey.*

25 TCR (@TeamCRonaldo), 'Cristiano Ronaldo: "I never tried to hide the fact that my only goal is to be the best",' Twitter, June 12, 2019, *https://twitter.com/teamcronaldo/status/1138740222940893186?lang=en.*

26 'Tomic to return to tennis but faces Davis Cup cold shoulder,' USA Today, published January 2018, *https://www.usatoday.com/story/sports/tennis/2018/01/30/tomic-to-return-to-tennis-but-faces-davis-cup-cold-shoulder/109958786/.*

27 Craig Ruvere, 'Respect Your Fellow Human Being – A Lesson American's Still Haven't Learned,' Craig Ruvere: The View from Here, published May 8, 2022, *https://craigruvere.com/respect-your-fellow-human-being/.*

28 Toni Mollett, 'Casey Stengel,' (brochure, Estate of Casey Stengel, 2010), https:*//caseystengel.org/wp-content/uploads/2010/11/stengel_brochure.pdf.*

29 Jim Schweigert, 'It's Amazing What You Can Accomplish When You Do Not Care Who Gets the Credit,' SeedWorld, published December 3, 2019, *https://seedworld.com/its-amazing-what-you-can-accomplish-when-you-do-not-care-who-gets-the-credit/#:~:text=President%20Harry%20Truman%20said%20it,the%20government%20could%20not%20succeed.*

30 Erin McCarthy, 'Roosevelt's "The Man in the Arena",' Mental Floss, published April 23, 2015, *https://www.mentalfloss.com/article/63389/roosevelts-man-arena.*

The author

Nathan started his career as a schoolteacher before the demands of AFL football took over. In a career that spanned seventeen seasons at St Kilda FC, he captured numerous individual awards while captaining his Club, his State, and representing Australia in the International Rules Series. His individual highlight was being awarded the AFL Hall of Fame Membership and Legend Status in the St Kilda Hall of Fame.

Post-football, Nathan has started his own consulting company which focuses on high performance, resilience and leadership. He juggles this role with coaching elite-level Women's AFL at the Western Bulldogs.

When he isn't imparting wisdom to parents, coaches and players at the grassroots level of sport, he loves nothing more than standing on the sidelines, supporting his three daughters.